THOMAS FULLER

Selections

THOMAS FULLER

Selections

With Essays by

CHARLES LAMB
LESLIE STEPHEN

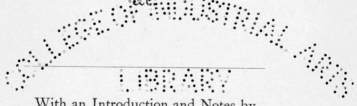
With an Introduction and Notes by
E. K. BROADUS

OXFORD
AT THE CLARENDON PRESS
1928

OXFORD UNIVERSITY PRESS
AMEN HOUSE E.C. 4
LONDON EDINBURGH GLASGOW
LEIPZIG NEW YORK TORONTO
MELBOURNE CAPETOWN BOMBAY
CALCUTTA MADRAS SHANGHAI
HUMPHREY MILFORD·
PUBLISHER TO THE
UNIVERSITY

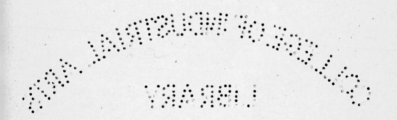

CONTENTS

INTRODUCTION

FULLER'S folios have long since been broken up into numerous volumes; but, even in this more usable form, they still make what Lamb called ' massy reading ', and to the pleasure-seeker their titles are as forbidding as their bulk. What reader would turn for delectation to six volumes of a *Church History* or three stout volumes (the *Worthies*) filled with half-page biographies of persons whose candle flickered out more than three centuries ago? Or who would seek lively reading in a collection of ' Characters ', illustrating ' The Good Wife ', ' The Good Husband ', ' The Good Widow ', ' The Good Landlord ', and more, under the heading of *The Holy State*? Surely these must be (the words are Fuller's) mere ' auxiliary books, only to be repaired-to on occasions ', or even ' such as are mere pieces of formality, so that if you look *on* them you look *through* them ; and he that peeps through the casement of the index, sees as much as if he were in the house '.

And then some light-hearted adventurer essays to turn a page or two of Fuller for the adventure's sake. Be it the *Church History*, or the *Worthies*, or *The Holy State*, or the *History of Cambridge*, or the *Pisgah-sight of Palestine*, or any one of half a dozen of the minor things, he discovers that no subject is so solemn or so dry, no compilation of a biography is so commonplace, but Fuller will lighten it with his gaiety, or mellow it with his charity, or irradiate it with his wit, or twist it with a quaint conceit. The sentence on ' auxiliary books ' is representative—and who but Fuller would have peeped through the casement of the index ?

Such a discovery may be made on any page ; but relish

for the unexpected, the sudden sally, the delightful irrelevance, is matter of temperament. Most of Fuller's contemporaries liked him enormously. It was an age of verbal
gymnastics and quick conceits. They liked puns, and Fuller
was the most inveterate of punsters. Nor did they prize
him merely for his tricks. They liked him because he could
be at once wise and merry. There was not much merriment
in the years between the appearance of Fuller's *Holy State*
in 1642 and his death on the 16th of August, 1661. His
genial books, masking under solemn titles, went to many
editions in those years. There is a delightful glimpse, which
Oldys [1] gives us from a seventeenth-century *Medley of
diverting Sayings, Stories, Characters, &c.*, of a meeting
between Fuller and Isaak Walton. Walton, too, liked to
mix in what he wrote, ' some innocent harmless mirth ; of
which, if thou be a severe, sour-complexioned man, then I
here disallow thee to be a competent judge '. Walton, so
the story goes, visited Fuller to secure materials for the life
of Richard Hooker. The *Church History* had just appeared.

' What do you think of it ? ' asked Fuller.

' I think ', replied Walton, ' that it should be acceptable
to all tempers, because there are *shades* in it for the warm,
and *sunshine* for those of a cold constitution. With youthful
readers, the facetious parts will be profitable to make the
serious more palatable, while reverend old readers will
fancy themselves in a flower garden, or one full of ever-
greens.'

' And why not the Church History so decked,' said Fuller,
' as well as the Church itself at a most Holy Season, or the
Tabernacle of old at the Feast of Boughs ? '

' That was but *for a season,*' Walton objected. ' In *your*
Feast of Boughs, we are so overshadowed that the parson

[1] In his article on Fuller in *Biographia Britannica*, iii, 1750, p.
2061.

is more seen than his congregation ; who may wander till they are lost in the labyrinth.'

' Oh,' said Fuller, ' the very *children* of our Israel may find their way out of *this* wilderness.'

' True,' returned Walton,' as indeed they have here such a Moses to conduct them.'

There are many such indications of contemporary liking for ' the great Tom Fuller '. Pepys pored over the *Church History* (while Mistress Pepys was deep in ' Great Cyrus ') till late at night ; or, after debating at his bookseller's on the claims of Chaucer, Stow, Shakespeare, or Jonson, ' at last chose Dr. Fuller's *Worthies* ', and spent next Easter day at home with his wife in ' pleasant talk and company one with another reading in Dr. Fuller's book '.

But in that day as in this there were not lacking severe sour-complexioned men who had no patience with a playful spirit. Dr. Heylin condemned Fuller's ' merry tales and scraps of Trencher-jests ', which ' neither do become the gravity of a Church-historian, nor are consistent with the nature of a sober argument '.[1] Bishop Nicolson said that the *Church History* was ' so interlac'd with Punn and Quibble, that it looks as if the Man had design'd to ridicule the Annals of our Church into Fable and Romance ', but added that ' if it were possible to refine it well, the work would be of good use '.[2]

In the eighteenth century Oldys thought that ' Dr. Fuller had some elegancies of style, but he indulged them till they diseased it ' ;[3] Bishop Warburton called him ' Fuller the Jester ' and said that he wrote ' in a style of buffoon pleasantry altogether unsuitable to so grave and

---

[1] *Examen Historicum*, 1659.

[2] *English Historical Library*, ed. 1736, p. 117.

[3] Oldys's manuscript notes in his copy of the *Worthies* as transcribed by George Steevens.

important a subject '.[1] Even as late as 1810 a writer in the *Edinburgh Review*[2] thinks that Fuller's ' quaint and anti-quated wit is perhaps more frequently found to disgust than to delight a fashionable age '.

The Edinburgh Reviewer was wrong. In the 1790's the *Gentleman's Magazine* began to quote Fuller and to suggest that there should be new editions. Southey professed that Fuller was his ' prime favourite author ', and enriched his Commonplace Books with copious extracts from *The Holy State* and the *Church History* and the *Worthies*. Then came Lamb, in whose merry and wayward fancy Fuller himself was reborn. It is not for nothing that the two writers to whom their contemporaries and posterity have applied the word ' quaint ' are Fuller and Charles Lamb. ' He was very kind, as he always was to young people, and very quaint', wrote one who as a boy had fallen under Lamb's spell. ' I told him that I had devoured his " Roast Pig ". He congratulated me on possessing a thorough schoolboy's appetite.' It is what Fuller might have said, and just what would have been said about him. It was Lamb (introducer of so many riches to the early nineteenth century) who first made Fuller generally known. Lamb's ' Specimens from the Writings of Thomas Fuller ' (taken chiefly from *The Holy State*) appeared in Leigh Hunt's *Reflector* in 1811. The same year saw the publication of John Nichols's reprint of the *Worthies*—and Fuller came into his own again.

Then Coleridge caught the infection (his notes are dated July 1829) ; and Lamb, stirred to renewed interest, bor-rowed the *Worthies* from Coleridge and rejoiced over it in letters to Gillman and Barton. Fuller delighted Lamb ; Coleridge was roused to enthusiasm. ' Next to Shakespeare ', he wrote, ' I am not certain whether Thomas Fuller, beyond

[1] *Directions for the Study of Theology*, Works, 1811, x. 371.
[2] Vol. iv, p. 96.

all other writers, does not excite in me the sense and emotion
of the marvellous : the degree in which any given faculty
or combination of faculties is possessed and manifested,
so far surpassing what one would have thought possible in
a single mind, as to give one's admiration the flavour and
quality of wonder ! . . . Fuller was incomparably the most
sensible, the *least* prejudiced, great man of an age that
boasted a galaxy of great men. He is a very voluminous
writer, and yet in all his numerous volumes on so many
different subjects, it is scarcely too much to say, that you
will hardly find a page in which some one sentence out of
every three does not deserve to be quoted for itself, as motto
or as maxim. *God bless thee*, dear old man ! May I meet with
thee ! which is tantamount to—may I go to Heaven ! '

It may be doubted whether Coleridge was not moved to
undue enthusiasm. We hesitate to rank Fuller's power
as next to Shakespeare's in exciting the sense of the
marvellous. The significance of Coleridge's outburst is that
no one can read Fuller without loving him. Coleridge's
' dear old man ' ; Lamb's ' dear fine silly old angel ' ; the
' quaint old Fuller ' of every enthusiastic discoverer, mark a
human and endearing quality. Among all English writers
only Lamb is so self-revealing. When we turn the opening
pages of any book of Fuller's, we are amused *at* him ; as we
read on, we are amused *with* him ; but by the time we have
turned the last page, he will have us by the heart-strings.
His ingenuity entertains, but it is his ingenuousness that
captivates. He will sacrifice anything—proportion, rele-
vance, continuity, anything but decency—for a good story.
He knows his besetting sin, and, in the act of sinning, he
exclaims : ' Forgive me, reader, though I would not write
these things they are so absurd, I cannot but write them
they are so absurd.' Or again : ' Reader, if the day be as
long with thee when thou readest, as it was with me when

I wrote, the ensuing story, time may be the better afforded
for the perusal thereof.'

It is characteristic too of his ingenuous spirit that even in
graver matters he never hesitates to take the reader into his
confidence. In that troubled time all men who were not
zealots or fanatics wished, as Fuller did, to ' tread fair and
softly ' ; but there were few so engagingly frank about it.
Church history, as it approached his own day, became
dangerous ground, comments on the notable controver-
sialists of the day a delicate matter. ' To say much in praise
or dispraise of them (wherein their relations are so nearly
concerned) may add too much to the writer's danger ' is a
thought that in one form or another falls frequently from
Fuller's pen. These deliberate evasions, and the fact that
he suffered less during the Commonwealth than many
Royalist divines, exposed him to the charge of pusillanimity
and ' trimming ' ; but in truth Fuller's life was an open
book. ' Had I poised myself so politickly betwixt both
parties that I had suffered from neither ', he writes in his
Good Thoughts in Bad Times, ' yet could I have took no contentment in my safe escaping.' He was unswervingly faithful
to his King and his Creed ; but peace, conciliation, toler-
ance, good feeling, were his watchwords. The *Appeal of
Injured Innocence*, in which he replies to Heylin's bitter
attack on the *Church History*, is an example of sustained
good temper and genial humour remarkable in an age when
theological controversy descended to ignoble personalities.
As for the letter ' To my Loving Friend, Dr. Peter Heylin',
which concludes the *Appeal*, Fuller's very self, quaint,
gentle, kindly, is compact in it. It is true that, man of his
time, Fuller disliked the Catholics. To write impartially
of them would have been to neglect his duty as a good
Churchman. He pointed many a moral, and indulged in
many a gibe, at their expense. He felt no inconsistency in

crediting the miracle of the King's Evil and at the same time discrediting the miracles of the *Legenda Aurea*. But, not infrequently, his liberal spirit gets the better of his professional prejudice. 'As for miracles which she wrought in her life-time', he writes of St. Hildegarde, 'their number is as admirable as their nature. I must confess, at my first reading of them, my belief digested some, but surfeited on the rest : for she made no more to cast out a devil, than a barber to draw a tooth, and with less pain to the patient. . . . However, Hildegardis was a gracious virgin, and God might perform some great wonders by her hand.'

It is not easy to do Fuller justice in a volume of selections. To collect his *obiter dicta* ; to display him in cap and bells ; to adopt Heylin's ironic suggestion that his 'merry tales and scraps of Trencher-jests' be 'put into a book by themselves' and 'served up for a second course to the *Banquet of Jests*, a supplement to the old book entitled *Wits, Fits and Fancies*, or an additional century to the old *Hundred Merry Tales*, so long since extant', would be to miss the best of him. Lamb's selections do little more than illustrate the liveliness of Fuller's fancy. Coleridge's 'one sentence out of every three . . . as motto or maxim' suggests the scrapbook. In such oddments Fuller's whimsical charm evaporates. His books, in truth, are good talk, the spontaneous overflow of a merry mind—and good talk requires leisure and a setting.

FULLER'S LIFE

1608. Thomas Fuller born at Aldwincle in Northamptonshire, in June.

1621. Entered Queens' College, Cambridge: B.A. 1625, M.A. 1628.

1630. Ordained; Perpetual Curate of St. Benet's Church, Cambridge, 1630–3.

1634. Rector of Broadwindsor, Dorsetshire, 1634–41.

1637. First marriage.

1639. *The Historie of the Holy Warre.*

1641. Settled in London, after his wife's death; Curate of the Savoy Chapel, 1641–3.

1642. *The Holy and Profane State.*

1643. Removed to Oxford (August), and settled at Lincoln College. Chaplain to Sir Ralph Hopton (about December).

1644. At Exeter; Chaplain to the Princess Henrietta Anne (born 16 June 1644).

1645. *Good Thoughts in Bad Times*, published at Exeter.

1646. Returned to London, after the surrender of Exeter to Fairfax.

1647. 'Lecturer' of the church of St. Clement's, Eastcheap. *Good Thoughts in Worse Times.*

1648 (or 49). Perpetual Curate of Waltham Abbey, and Chaplain to the Earl of Carlisle.

1650. *A Pisgah-sight of Palestine.*

1651. *Abel Redevivus.*
Second marriage—to Mary Roper, daughter of Viscount Baltinglass.
'Lecturer' again at St. Clement's, Eastcheap, 1651–4.

1655. *The Church-History of Britain.*
The History of the University of Cambridge.
The History of Waltham-Abbey in Essex.
Chaplain to George Berkeley, who succeeded as Baron Berkeley; afterwards created Earl of Berkeley.

1658. Rector of Cranford, Middlesex, 1658–61.

1659. *The Appeal of Injured Innocence*, in answer to Peter Heylyn's *Examen Historicum.*

1660. *Mixt Contemplations in Better Times* (February).
Accompanied Lord Berkeley to the Hague (May).
After the Restoration of Charles II, 'invited to his former Lecturer's place at the Savoy'.

1661. Chaplain in extraordinary to the King.
Died at his lodgings in Covent Garden of a violent fever, 16 August; buried in Cranford Church 17 August.
1662. *The History of the Worthies of England* published by 'the author's orphan' John Fuller.

LATER EDITIONS

The Holy State, and the Profane State.
Ed. James Nichols, 1 vol. octavo, 1841.
The Church-History of Britain.
Ed. James Nichols, 3 vols. octavo, 1837.
Ed. J. S. Brewer, 6 vols. octavo, Oxford 1845.
The History of the Worthies of England.
Ed. John Nichols, 2 vols. folio, 1811.
Ed. P. A. Nuttall, 3 vols. octavo, 1840.

BIOGRAPHY

The Life of Thomas Fuller, D.D. With Notices of His Books, His Kinsmen, and His Friends. By John Eglington Bailey. 1874.

THE LIFE OF

DR. THOMAS FULLER.

London, 1661 (Anonymous)

WITH the progress of the War he marched from place to
place, and where ever there happened for the better accommodation of the Army any reasonable stay, he allotted it
with great satisfaction to his beloved studies. Those cessa-
tions and intermissions, begot in him the most intentnesse
and sollicitous industry of mind, which as he never used to
much recreation or diversion in times of peace, which might
loose and relasch a well disciplin'd spirit ; so neither did the
horrour and rigidnesse of the war stiffen him in such a
stupidity (which generally possest all Learned Men) or else 10
distract him, but that in such lucid intervals, he would
seriously and fixedly come to himself and his designed
businesse.

Indeed his businesse and study then, was a kind of Er-
rantry, having proposed to himself a more exact Collection
of the *Worthies General* of *England*, in which others had
waded before, but he resolved to go through. In what place
soever therefore he came, of remark especially, he spent
frequently most of his time in views and researches of their
Antiquities and Church-Monuments, insinuating himself 20
into the acquaintance (which frequently ended in a lasting
friendship) of the learnedst and gravest persons residing
within the place, thereby to informe himself fully of those
things he thought worthy the commendation of his labours.
It is an incredible thing to think what a numerous corre-
spondence the Doctor maintained and enjoyed by this
means.

Nor did the good Doctor ever refuse to light his Candle in investigating Truth from the meanest persons discovery. He would endure contentedly an hours or more impertinence from any aged Church-officer, or other superannuated people for the gleaning of two lines to his purpose. And though his spirit was quick and nimble, and all the faculties of his mind ready and answerable to that activity of dispatch, yet in these inquests he would stay and attend those *circular* rambles till they came to a *poynt*; so resolute was he bent to the sifting out of abstruse Antiquity. Nor did he ever dismisse any such feeble Adjutators or Helpers (as he pleased to style them) without giving them money and chearful thanks besides. . . .

In the Interim came out a Book of Dr. *Heylins*, called *Animadversions upon Mr.* Fuller's *Ecclesiastical History*, wherein somewhat tartly (though with that judicious learning for which that *Doctor* is most deservedly honoured) he taxed that Book of some Errors, *&c.* To this the *Doctor* replyed by a Book styled *The Appeal of injured Innocence to the learned and ingenious Reader*, being a very modest but a most rational and polite defence to the aforesaid exceptions against that elaborate Piece. The *Dispute* and *Controversie* was soon ended, the Oyl the *Doctor* bestowed on this labour, being poured into the fresh Wound of this Quarrel did so asswage the heat of the *Contest*, that it was soon healed into a perfect amicable closure and mutual endearment.

Indeed the grace that was supereminent in the good *Doctor* was Charity, both in giving and forgiving; as he had laboured during our civil broils after peace, so when that could not through our sins be attained, did he with the same earnestnesse presse the *Duty* of Love, especially among Brethren of the same afflicted and too much already divided

Church ; and therefore was most exemplary in keeping the band of it himself, though in a matter that most nearly concerned his credit and fame, the chiefest worldly Thing he studied and intended.

This constrained retrospection of the *Doctors* to secure and assist the far advanced strength of his foremost works, did a little retard and impede the arriere of his labours, which consisted of the flower and choice of all his Abilities and wherein his *WORTHIES* were placed ; howbeit this proved but a Halt, to those encumbrances and difficulties, which he had all along before met, and soon set that Book on foot again.

This was the last *Remora* to it, the *Doctor* going on a smooth swift pace while all things else were retrograde in the Kingdome, through the tyrannical plots and stratagems of the *Usurper Cromwel* ; so as toward the beginning of that *mirabilis Annus* 1660 he had it ready for the *Press*, to which assoon as the wonders of his *Majesties* Restitution was over, (in the thankful contemplation whereof the good Doctor was so piously fixt as nothing else might presume to intrude upon his raised gladded spirits) he brought it, taking the *auspicia* of that happy and famous juncture of time for the Commencement of this Everlasting Monument of himself as well, as all other English Noble deceased Persons.

A while before to compleat the Doctor's contentment as to his Ministry also, he was invited to his former Lecturers place at the *Savoy*, who even from his departure had suffered under an insufficient or disloyal and malicious Clergy ; and therefore stood in need of an able and dutiful Son of the *Church* to reduce and lead them in the right way and the old paths ; For this *People* (his ancient flock) the Doctor had alwayes a more especial respect and kindnesse, which was the rather heightned in him out of a compassion to their state and condition. Nor did he more tenderly affect them then they universally respect him, receiving him (as indeed he was) as an Angel of God, sent to minister unto them heavenly things, in exchange whereof they freely gave him their hearts and hands.

The Doctor through the injury and iniquity of the times had for neer 20 years been barred of all *Profits* of his Prebendariship of *Salisbury* (of which before,) but upon the return of the *King*, those Revenues and Possessions so
10 sacrilegiously alienated from the Church, reverted also to their rightful Proprietors. This accession and additional Help did very much encourage the Doctor in the carrying on of his Book, which being large would require an able *Purse* to go through with, and he was very solicitous, (often presaging he should not live to see it finished though satisfied of his present healthy constitution) to have it done out of hand ; to which purpose part of the Money accrewing to him from his *Salisbury* Prebendariship was designed.

20 He therefore hastned his Book with all Expedition, and whereas he had intended to continue it but till 1659 and had therefore writ it in such language as those times of *Usurpation* (during the most part of which it was compiled) would suffer such a subject and concerning Matter to be drest in ; he now reviewed it over, giving Truth, and his own most excellent Phansie their proper becoming Ornaments, *Scope* and *Clearnesse*. But neither the elevation of the *Usurpers*, nor the depression of the *Royallists*, and the *Vice-versa* of it did ever incline or sway him to additions,
30 intercalations or expunctions of persons, whom he hath recommended to the world for *Worthies* ; no such thing as a *Pym* or *Protector* whom the mad world cryed up for *Brave* : Drops of compassionate tears they did force from him, but his resolute *Inke* was not to be stained by their *black* actions.

A Pen full of such, would serve to blot out the whole Roll of Fame.

This constancy of the Doctors to his first model and main of his design doth most evidently argue his firm perswasion and belief of the reviving of the *Royall Cause*, since he wrote the most part during those improbable times of any Restitution ; and he had very ill consulted his own advantage if he had not well consulted the Oracles of God.

As the last felicity of this Doctors life, he was made Chaplain in Extraordinary to his *Majesty*, being also in a 10 well grounded expectation of some present further advancement ; but here Death stept in and drew the Curtain betwixt him, and his succeeding Ecclesiastical Dignities. . . .

He was of Stature somewhat Tall, exceeding the meane, with a proportionable bigness to become it, but no way inclining to Corpulency : of an exact Straightnesse of the whole Body, and a perfect Symmetry in every part thereof. He was of a Sanguine constitution, which beautified his Face with a pleasant Ruddinesse, but of so Grave and serious an aspect, that it Awed and Discountenanced the 20 smiling Attracts of that complexion. His Head Adorned with a comely Light-Coloured Haire, which was so, by Nature exactly Curled (an Ornament enough of it self in this Age to Denominate a handsome person, and wherefore all Skill and Art is used) but not suffered to overgrow to any length unseeming his modesty and Profession.

His Gate and Walking was very upright and graceful, becoming his well shapen Bulke : approaching something near to that we terme Majesticall ; but that the Doctor was so well known to be void of any affectation or pride. 30 Nay so Regardlesse was he of himselfe in his Garb and Rayment, in which no doubt his Vanity would have appeared, as well as in his stately pace : that it was with some trouble to himselfe, to be either Neat or Decent ; it matter'd not for the outside, while he thought himself never too Curious and Nice in the Dresses of his mind.

Very Carelesse also he was to seeming inurbanity in the modes of Courtship and demeanour, deporting himself much according to the old *English* Guise, which for its ease and simplicity suited very well with the Doctor, whose time was designed for more Elaborate businesse : and whose MOTTO might have been sincerity.

10 As inobservant he was of persons, unlesse businesse with them ; or his concerns pointed them out and adverted him ; seeing and discerning were two things : often in several places, hath he met with Gentlemen of his nearest and great-est Acquaintance, at a full rencounter and stop, whom he hath endeavoured to passe by, not knowing, that is to say, not minding of them, till rectifyed and recalled by their familiar compellations.

This will not (it may be presumed) and justly cannot be imputed unto any indisposednesse and unaptnesse of his 20 Nature, which was so far from Rude and untractable, that it may be confidently averred, he was the most complacent person in the Nation, as his Converse and Writings, with such a freedome of Discourse and quick Jocundity of style, do sufficiently evince.

He was a perfect walking Library, and those that would finde delight in him must turn him ; he was to be diverted from his present purpose with some urgency : and when once Unfixed and Unbent, his mind freed from the incumbency of his Study ; no Man could be more agreeable to Civil and 30 Serious mirth, which limits his most heightned Fancy never transgressed.

He had the happinesse of a very Honourable, and that very numerous acquaintance, so that he was no way un-disciplined in the Arts of Civility ; yet he continued *semper idem*, which constancy made him alwaies acceptable to them.

At his Diet he was very sparing and temperate, but yet he allowed himself the repasts and refreshings of two Meals a day : but no lover of Dainties, or the Inventions of Cookery : solid meats better fitting his strength of Constitution ; but from drink very much abstemious, which questionlesse was the cause of that uninterrupted Health he enjoyed till this his First and Last sicknesse : of which Felicity as he himself was partly the cause of by his exact- 10 nesse in eating and drinking, so did he the more dread the sudden infliction of any Disease, or other violence of Nature, fearing this his care might amount to a presumption, in the Eyes of the great Disposer of all things, and so it pleased GOD it should happen.

But his great abstinence of all was from Sleep, and strange it was that one of such a Fleshly and sanguine composition, could overwatch so many heavy propense inclinations to Rest. For this in some sort he was beholden to his care in Diet aforesaid, (the full Vapours of a repletion in the 20 Stomack ascending to the Brain, causing that usual Drowsinesse we see in many) but most especially to his continual custome, use, and practise, which had so subdued his Nature, that it was wholy Governed by his Active and Industrious mind.

And yet this is a further wonder : he did scarcely allow himself, from his First Degree in the University any Recreation or Easie Exercise, no not so much as walking, but very Rare and Seldome ; and that not upon his own choice, but as being compelled by friendly, yet, Forcible Invitations ; till such time as the War posted him from place to place, 30 and after that his constant attendance on the Presse in the Edition of his Books : when was a question, which went the fastest, his Head or his Feet : so that in effect he was a very stranger, if not an Enemy to all pleasure.

Riding was the most pleasant, because his necessary convenience; the Doctors occasions, especially his last work, requiring Travel, to which he had so accustomed himself; so that this Diversion, (like Princes Banquets only to be lookt upon by them, not tasted of) was rather made such then enjoyed by him.

So that if there were any Felicity or Delight, which he can be truly said to have had: it was either in his Relations or in his Works. As to his Relations, certainly, no man was more a tender, more indulgent a Husband and a Father: his Conjugal Love in both matches being equally blest with the same Issue, kept a constant Tenour in both Marriages, which he so improved, that the Harmony of his Affections still'd all Discord, and Charmed the noyse of passion.

Towards the Education of his Children, he was exceeding carefull, allowing them any thing conducing to that end, beyond the present measure of his estate; which its well hoped will be returned to the Memory of so good a Father, in their early imitation of him in all those good Qualities and Literature, to which they have now such an Hereditary clayme.

As to his Books, which we usually call the Issue of the Brain, he was more then Fond, totally abandoning and forsaking all things to follow them. And yet if Correction and Severity (so this may be allowed the gravity of the Subject) be also the signes of Love: a stricter and more carefull hand was never used. True it is they did not grow up without some errours, like the Tares: nor can the most refined pieces of any of his Antagonists boast of perfection. He that goes an unknown and beaten Track in a Dubious way, though he may have good directions, yet if in the journey he chance to stray, cannot well be blamed; they have perchance plowed with his Heifer, and been beholden to those Authorities (for their Exceptions) which he first gave light to.

To his Neighbours and Friends he behaved himselfe with that chearfulnesse and plainnesse of Affection and respect, as deservedly gained him their Highest esteeme : from the meanest to the highest he omitted nothing what to him belonged in his station, either in a familiar correspondency, or necessary Visits : never suffering intreaties of that which either was his Duty, or in his power to perform. The quickness of his apprehension helped by a Good Nature, presently suggested unto him (without putting them to the trouble of an *innuendo*) what their severall Affairs required, in 10 which he would spare no paynes : insomuch that it was a piece of Absolute Prudence to rely upon his Advice and Assistance. In a word, to his Superiours he was Dutifully respectfull without Ceremony or Officiousnesse ; to his equalls he was Discreetly respectful ; without neglect or unsociableness, and to his Inferiours, (whom indeed he judged Christianly none to be) civilly respectfull without Pride or Disdain.

But all these so eminent vertues, and so sublimed in him were but as foyles to those excellent gifts wherewith God 20 had endued his intellectuals. He had a memory of that vast comprehensiveness, that he is deservedly known for the first inventer of that Noble Art, whereof having left behind him no Rules, or directions, save, onely what fell from him in discours, no further account can be given, but a relation of some very rare experiments of it made by him.

He undertook once in passing to and fro from *Temple-bar* to the furthest Conduit in *Cheapside*, at his return again to tell every Signe as they stood in order on both sides of the way, repeating them either backward or forward, as they 30 should chuse, which he exactly did, not missing or misplacing one, to the admiration of those that heard him.

The like also would he doe in words of different Languages, and of hard and difficult prolation, to any number whatsoever : but that which was most strange, and very rare in him, was his way of writing, which something like the *Chineses*, was from the top of the page to the bottom : the manner thus. He would write near the Margin the first words of every Line down to the Foot of the Paper, then would he, beginning at the head againe, fill up every one of these Lines, which without any interlineations or spaces but with the full and equal length, would so adjust the sense and matter, and so aptly Connex and Conjoyn the ends and beginnings of the said Lines, that he could not do it better, as he hath said, if he had writ all out in a Continuation.

The Treasury of this Happy Memory was a very great Advantage to his Preaching : but being assisted with as Rich invention, and extraordinary reading, did absolutely compleat him for the Pulpit. His great stores both of Schoole and case Divinity, both of History and Philosophy, of Arts and Tongues, his Converse in the Scriptures, the Fathers and Humane Writings had so abundantly furnished him, that without the other additaments he had been very eminent among his function. Now all so happily met together ; such a Constellation could portend no lesse then some wonder of men, who should be Famous in his Generation.

SAMUEL PEPYS on FULLER

Extracts from the Diary

7th Dec. 1660. I fell a-reading Fuller's History of Abbeys, and my wife in Great Cyrus, till twelve at night, and so to bed.

5th Jan. 1660/61. Home all the morning. Several people came to me about business, among others the great Tom Fuller, who came to desire a kindness for a friend of his who

hath a mind to go to Jamaica with these two ships that are
going, which I promised to do.

22nd Jan. 1660/61. I met with Dr. Thomas Fuller, and
took him to the Dog, where he tells me of his last and great
book that is coming out : that is, the History of all the
Families in England ; and could tell me more of my own,
than I knew myself. And also to what perfection he hath
now brought the art of memory ; that he did lately to four
eminently great scholars dictate together in Latin, upon
different subjects of their proposing, faster than they were
able to write, till they were tired : and that the best way
of beginning a sentence, if a man should be out and forget
his last sentence (which he never was) that then his last
refuge is to begin with an *utcunque*.

3rd Feb. (Lord's Day) 1660/61. This day I first begun to
go forth in my coat and sword, as the manner now among
gentlemen is. To White Hall. In my way heard Mr. Thomas
Fuller preach at the Savoy upon our forgiving of other
men's trespasses, shewing among other things that we are
to go to law never to revenge, but only to repair, which I
think a good distinction.

12th May 1661. At the Savoy heard Dr. Fuller preach
upon David's words, ' I will wait with patience all the days
of my appointed time until my change comes ' ; but me-
thought it was a poor dry sermon. And I am afraid my
former high esteem of his preaching was more out of opinion
than judgment.

10th Feb. 1661/2. Musique practice a good while, then
to Paul's Churchyard, and there I met with Dr. Fuller's
England's Worthies ; the first time that I ever saw it ; and
so I sat down reading in it, till it was two o'clock before I
thought of the time going ; and so I rose and went home to
dinner, being much troubled that (though he had some
discourse with me about my family and arms) he says

nothing at all, nor mentions us either in Cambridgeshire or Norfolk. But I believe indeed our family were never considerable.

23rd Feb. 1662. My cold being increased, I stayed at home all day, pleasing myself with my dining-room, now graced with pictures, and reading of Dr. Fuller's Worthies : so I spent the day.

10th Dec. 1663. To St. Paul's Churchyard, to my bookseller's, and having gained this day in the office by my stationer's bill to the King about 40s. or £3, I did here sit two or three hours calling for twenty books to lay this money out upon, and found myself at a great loss where to choose, and do see how my nature would gladly return to the laying out money in this trade. I could not tell whether to lay out my money for books of pleasure, as plays, which my nature was most earnest in ; but at last after seeing Chaucer, Dugdale's History of Paul's, Stow's London, Gesner, History of Trent, besides Shakespeare, Jonson, and Beaumont's plays, I at last chose Dr. Fuller's Worthies, The Cabbala or Collections of Letters of State, and a little book Delices de Hollande, with another little book or two, all of good use or serious pleasure ; and Hudibras, both parts, the book now in greatest fashion for drollery, though I cannot, I confess, see enough where the wit lies.

10th April (Lord's Day) 1664. Lay long in bed and then up and my wife dressed herself, it being Easter day, but I not being so well as to go out, she, though much against her will, stayed at home with me. . . . We spent the day in pleasant talk and company one with another, reading in Dr. Fuller's book what he says of the Cliffords and Kingsmills.

CHARLES LAMB on FULLER

Specimens from the Writings of Fuller, the Church Historian

(*The Reflector*, No. IV, 1811 ; *Works*, 1818)

THE writings of Fuller are usually designated by the title of quaint, and with sufficient reason ; for such was his natural bias to conceits, that I doubt not upon most occasions it would have been going out of his way to have expressed himself out of them. But his wit is not always a *lumen siccum*, a dry faculty of surprising ; on the contrary, his conceits are oftentimes deeply steeped in human feeling and passion. Above all, his way of telling a story, for its eager liveliness, and the perpetual running commentary of the narrator happily blended with the narration, is perhaps unequalled.

As his works are now scarcely perused but by antiquaries I thought it might not be unacceptable to my readers to present them with some specimens of his manner, in single thoughts and phrases ; and in some few passages of greater length, chiefly of a narrative description. I shall arrange them as I casually find them in my book of extracts, without being solicitous to specify the particular work from which they are taken.

Pyramids.—' The Pyramids themselves, doting with age, have forgotten the names of their founders.'

Virtue in a short person.—' His soul had but a short diocese to visit, and therefore might the better attend the effectual informing thereof.'

Intellect in a very tall one.—' Oft times such who are built four stories high, are observed to have little in their cockloft.'

Naturals.—' Their heads sometimes so little, that there is no room for wit ; sometimes so long, that there is no wit for so much room.'

Negroes.—' The image of God cut in ebony.'

School-divinity.—' At the first it will be as welcome to thee as a prison, and their very solutions will seem knots unto thee.'

Mr. Perkins, the Divine.—' He had a capacious head, with angles winding and roomy enough to lodge all controversial intricacies.'

The same.—' He would pronounce the word *Damn* with such an emphasis as left a doleful echo in his auditors' ears a good while after.'

Judges in capital cases.—' O let him take heed how he strikes, that hath a dead hand.'

Memory.—' Philosophers place it in the rear of the head, and it seems the mine of memory lies there, because there men naturally dig for it, scratching it when they are at a loss.'

Fancy.—' It is the most boundless and restless faculty of the soul ; for while the Understanding and the Will are kept, as it were, *in libera custodia* to their objects of *verum et bonum*, the Fancy is free from all engagements : it digs without spade, sails without ship, flies without wings, builds without charges, fights without bloodshed ; in a moment striding from the centre to the circumference of the world ; by a kind of omnipotency creating and annihilating things in an instant ; and things divorced in Nature are married in Fancy as in a lawless place.'

Infants.—' Some, admiring what motives to mirth infants meet with in their silent and solitary smiles, have resolved, how truly I know not, that then they converse with angels ; as indeed such cannot among mortals find any fitter companions.'

Music.—' Such is the sociableness of music, it conforms

itself to all companies both in mirth and mourning ; complying to improve that passion with which it finds the auditors most affected. In a word, it is an invention which might have beseemed a son of Seth to have been the father thereof : though better it was that Cain's great grandchild should have the credit first to find it, than the world the unhappiness longer to have wanted it.'

St. Monica.—' Drawing near her death, she sent most pious thoughts as harbingers to heaven, and her soul saw a glimpse of happiness through the chinks of her sickness- [10] broken body.' [1]

Mortality.—' To smell to a turf of fresh earth is wholesome for the body, no less are thoughts of mortality cordial to the soul.'

Virgin.—' No lording husband shall at the same time command her presence and distance ; to be always near in constant attendance, and always to stand aloof in awful observance.'

Elder Brother.—' Is one who made haste to come into the world to bring his parents the first news of male posterity, [20] and is well rewarded for his tidings.'

Bishop Fletcher.—' His pride was rather on him than in him, as only gait and gesture deep, not sinking to his heart, though causelessly condemned for a proud man, as who was a *good hypocrite*, and far more humble than he appeared.'

Masters of Colleges.—' A little allay of dulness in a Master of a College makes him fitter to manage secular affairs.'

The Good Yeoman.—' Is a gentleman in ore, whom the next age may see refined.'

Good Parent.—' For his love, therein, like a well-drawn [30] picture, he eyes all his children alike.'

---

[1] The soul's dark cottage, batter'd and decay'd,
  Lets in new lights through chinks which time has made.—
                                        WALLER.

Deformity in Children.—' This partiality is tyranny, when parents despise those that are deformed ; *enough to break those whom God had bowed before.*'

Good Master.—' In correcting his servant he becomes not a slave to his own passion. Not cruelly making new *indentures* of the flesh of his apprentice. He is tender of his servant in sickness and age. If crippled in his service, his house is his hospital. Yet how many throw away those dry bones, out of the which themselves have sucked the marrow ! '

Good Widow.—' If she can speak but little good of him [her dead husband] she speaks but little of him. So handsomely folding up her discourse, that his virtues are shewn outwards, and his vices wrapt up in silence ; as counting it barbarism to throw dirt on his memory who hath moulds cast on his body.'

Horses.—' These are men's wings, wherewith they make much speed. A generous creature a horse is, sensible in some sort of honour ; and made most handsome by that which deforms men most—pride.'

Martyrdom.—' Heart of oak hath sometime warped a little in the scorching heat of persecution. Their want of true courage herein cannot be excused. Yet many censure them for surrendering up their forts after a long siege, who would have yielded up their own at the first summons. Oh ! there is more required to make one valiant, than to call Cranmer or Jewel coward ; as if the fire in Smithfield had been no hotter than what is painted in the Book of Martyrs.'

Text of St. Paul.—' St. Paul saith, let not the sun go down on your wrath, to carry news to the antipodes in another world of thy revengeful nature. Yet let us take the Apostle's meaning rather than his words, with all possible speed to depose our passion ; not understanding him so literally, that we may take leave to be angry till sunset : then might our wrath lengthen with the days ; and men in Greenland, where the day lasts above a quarter of a year, have plentiful scope for revenge.' [1]

Bishop Brownrig.—' He carried learning enough *in numerato* about him in his pockets for any discourse, and had much more at home in his chests for any serious dispute.'

Modest Want.—' Those that with diligence fight against poverty, though neither conquer till death makes it a drawn battle ; expect not but prevent their craving of thee : for God forbid the heavens should never rain, till the earth first opens her mouth ; seeing *some grounds will sooner burn than chap.*'

Death-bed Temptations.—' The devil is most busy on the last day of his term ; and a tenant to be outed cares not what mischief he doth.'

Conversation.—' Seeing we are civilized Englishmen, let us not be naked savages in our talk.'

Wounded Soldier.—' Halting is the stateliest march of a soldier ; and 'tis a brave sight to see the flesh of an ancient as torn as his colours.'

Wat Tyler.—' *A misogrammatist ;* if a good Greek word may be given to so barbarous a rebel.'

Heralds.—' Heralds new mould men's names,—taking from them, adding to them, melting out all the liquid letters, torturing mutes to make them speak, and making vowels dumb,—to bring it to a fallacious *homonomy* at the last,

---

[1] This whimsical prevention of a consequence which no one would have thought of deducing,—setting up an absurdum on purpose to hunt it down,—placing guards as it were at the very outposts of possibility,—gravely giving out laws to insanity and prescribing moral fences to distempered intellects, could never have entered into a head less entertainingly constructed than that of Fuller, or Sir Thomas Browne, the very air of whose style the conclusion of this passage aptly imitates.

that their names may be the same with those noble houses they pretend to.'

Antiquarian Diligence.—' It is most worthy observation, with what diligence he [Camden] enquired after ancient places, making hue and cry after many a city which was run away, and by certain marks and tokens pursuing to find it ; as by the situation on the Roman highways, by just distance from other ancient cities, by some affinity of name, by tradition of the inhabitants, by Roman coins digged up, and by some appearance of ruins. A broken urn is a whole evidence ; or an old gate still surviving, out of which the city is run out. Besides, commonly some new spruce town not far off is grown out of the ashes thereof, which yet hath so much natural affection as dutifully to own those reverend ruins for her mother.'

Henry de Essex.—' He is too well known in our English Chronicles, being Baron of Raleigh, in Essex, and Hereditary Standard Bearer of England. It happened in the reign of this king [Henry II.] there was a fierce battle fought in Flintshire, at Coleshull, between the English and Welsh, wherein this Henry de Essex *animum et signum simul abjecit*, betwixt traitor and coward cast away both his courage and banner together, occasioning a great overthrow of English. But he that had the baseness to do, had the boldness to deny the doing of so foul a fact ; until he was challenged in combat by Robert de Momford, a knight, eye-witness thereof, and by him overcome in a duel. Whereupon his large inheritance was confiscated to the king, and he himself, *partly thrust, partly going into a convent, hid his head in a cowl, under which, betwixt shame and sanctity, he blushed out the remainder of his life.'* [1]—Worthies. Article, Bedfordshire.

---

[1] The fine imagination of Fuller has done what might have been pronounced impossible : it has given an interest, and a holy character, to coward infamy. Nothing can be more beautiful than the

Sir Edward Harwood, Knt.—' I have read of a bird, which hath a face like, and yet will prey upon, a man ; who coming to the water to drink, and finding there by reflection, that he had killed one like himself, pineth away by degrees, and never afterwards enjoyeth itself.[1] Such is in some sort the condition of Sir Edward. This accident, that he had killed one in a private quarrel, put a period to his carnal mirth, and was a covering to his eyes all the days of his life. No possible provocations could afterwards tempt him to a duel ; and no wonder that one's conscience loathed that whereof he had surfeited. He refused all challenges with more honour than others accepted them ; it being well known, that he

concluding account of the last days, and expiatory retirement, of poor Henry de Essex. The address with which the whole of this little story is told is most consummate : the charm of it seems to consist in a perpetual balance of antitheses not too violently opposed, and the consequent activity of mind in which the reader is kept :— ' Betwixt traitor and coward '—' baseness to do, boldness to deny '— ' partly thrust, partly going, into a convent '—' betwixt shame and sanctity '. The reader by this artifice is taken into a kind of partner-ship with the writer,—his judgment is exercised in settling the pre-ponderance,—he feels as if he were consulted as to the issue. But the modern historian flings at once the dead weight of his own judgment into the scale, and settles the matter.

[1] I do not know where Fuller read of this bird ; but a more awful and affecting story, and moralizing of a story, in Natural History, or rather in that Fabulous Natural History, where poets and mytho-logists found the Phœnix and the Unicorn, and ' other strange fowl ', is no where extant. It is a fable which Sir Thomas Browne, if he had heard of it, would have exploded among his Vulgar Errors ; but the delight which he would have taken in the discussing of its probabilities, would have shewn that the *truth of the fact*, though the avowed object of his search, was not so much the motive which put him upon the investigation, as those hidden affinities and poetical analogies,—those *essential verities* in the application of strange fable, which made him linger with such reluctant delay among the last fading lights of popular tradition ; and not seldom to conjure up a superstition, that had been long extinct, from its dusty grave, to inter it himself with greater ceremonies and solemnities of burial.

would set his foot as far in the face of his enemy as any man alive.'—*Worthies. Art. Lincolnshire.*

Decayed Gentry.—' It happened in the reign of King James, when Henry Earl of Huntingdon was Lieutenant of Leicestershire, that a labourer's son in that county was pressed into the wars; as I take it, to go over with Count Mansfield. The old man at Leicester requested his son might be discharged, as being the only staff of his age, who by his industry maintained him and his mother. The Earl de-10 manded his name, which the man for a long time was loth to tell (as suspecting it a fault for so poor a man to confess the truth), at last he told his name was Hastings. " Cousin Hastings," said the Earl, " we cannot all be top branches of the tree, though we all spring from the same root ; your son, my kinsman, shall not be pressed." So good was the meeting of modesty in a poor, with courtesy in an honourable person, and gentry I believe in both. And I have reason to believe, that some who justly own the surnames and blood of Bohuns, Mortimers, and Plantagenets (though 20 ignorant of their own extractions), are hid in the heap of common people, where they find that under a thatched cottage, which some of their ancestors could not enjoy in a leaded castle,—contentment, with quiet and security.'— *Worthies. Art. Of Shire-Reeves or Shiriffes.*

Tenderness of Conscience in a Tradesman.—' Thomas Curson, born in Allhallows, Lombard-street, armourer, dwelt without Bishopsgate. It happened that a stage-player borrowed a rusty musket, which had laid long leger in his shop : now though his part were comical, he there-30 with acted an unexpected tragedy, killing one of the standers by, the gun casually going off on the stage, which he suspected not to be charged. O the difference of divers men in the tenderness of their consciences ; some are scarce touched with a wound, whilst others are wounded with a touch therein. This poor armourer was highly afflicted therewith, though done against his will, yea without his knowledge, in his absence, by another, out of mere chance. Hereupon he resolved to give all his estate to pious uses : no sooner had he gotten a round sum, but presently he posted with it in his apron to the Court of Aldermen, and was in pain till by their direction he had settled it for the relief of poor in his own and other parishes, and disposed of some hundreds of pounds accordingly, as I am credibly informed by the then churchwardens of the said parish. Thus as he conceived himself casually (though at a great distance) to have occasioned the death of one, he was the immediate and direct cause of giving a comfortable living to many.'

Burning of Wickliffe's Body by Order of the Council of Constance.—' Hitherto [A. D. 1428] the corpse of John Wickliffe had quietly slept in his grave about forty-one years after his death, till his body was reduced to bones, and his bones almost to dust. For though the earth in the chancel of Lutterworth, in Leicestershire, where he was interred, hath not so quick a digestion with the earth of Aceldama, to consume flesh in twenty-four hours, yet such the appetite thereof, and all other English graves, to leave small reversions of a body after so many years. But now such the spleen of the Council of Constance, as they not only cursed his memory as dying an obstinate heretic, but ordered that his bones (with this charitable caution,—if it may be discerned from the bodies of other faithful people) be taken out of the ground, and thrown far off from any Christian burial. In obedience hereunto, Rich. Fleming, Bishop of Lincoln, Diocesan of Lutterworth, sent his officers (vultures with a quick sight, scent, at a dead carcase) to ungrave him. Accordingly to Lutterworth they come, Sumner, Commissary, Official, Chancellor, Proctors, Doctors, and their servants (so that the remnant of the body would not hold out a bone amongst so many hands), take what was left out of the grave, and burnt them to ashes, and cast them into Swift, a neighbouring brook, running hard by. *Thus this brook has conveyed his ashes into Avon, Avon into Severn, Severn into the narrow seas, they into the main ocean ; and thus the ashes of Wickliffe are the emblem of his doctrine, which now is dispersed all the world over.'* [1]—Church History.

[1] The concluding period of this most lively narrative I will not call a conceit : it is one of the grandest conceptions I ever met with. One feels the ashes of Wickliffe gliding away out of the reach of the Sumners, Commissaries, Officials, Proctors, Doctors, and all the puddering rout of executioners of the impotent rage of the baffled Council : from Swift into Avon, from Avon into Severn, from Severn into the narrow seas, from the narrow seas into the main ocean, where they become the emblem of his doctrine, ' dispersed all the world over.' Hamlet's tracing the body of Cæsar to the clay that stops a beer-barrel, is a no less curious pursuit of ' ruined mortality ' ; but it is in an inverse ratio to this : it degrades and saddens us, for one part of our nature at least ; but this expands the whole of our nature, and gives to the body a sort of ubiquity,—a diffusion, as far as the actions of its partner can have reach or influence.

I have seen this passage smiled at, and set down as a quaint conceit of old Fuller. But what is not a conceit to those who read it in a temper different from that in which the writer composed it ? The most pathetic parts of poetry to cold tempers seem and are nonsense, as divinity was to the Greeks foolishness. When Richard II, meditating on his own utter annihilation as to royalty, cries out,

> ' O that I were a mockery king of snow,
> To melt before the sun of Bolingbroke,'

if we have been going on pace for pace with the passion before, this sudden conversion of a strong-felt metaphor into something to be actually realized in nature, like that of Jeremiah, ' Oh ! that my head were waters, and mine eyes a fountain of tears,' is strictly and strikingly natural ; but come unprepared upon it, and it is a conceit ; and so is a ' head ' turned into ' waters '.

[We are too apt to indemnify ourselves for some characteristic excellence we are kind enough to concede to a great author, by denying him everything else. Thus Donne and Cowley, by happening to possess more wit and faculty of illustration than other men,

Extracts from Letters

To James Gillman.

November 29, 1829.

Pray trust me with the ' Church History ' and the ' Worthies '. A moon shall restore both. Also give me back Him of Aquinum. In return you have the light of my countenance. . . .

From my country lodgings at Enfield.   C. L.

To James Gillman.

November 30, 1829.

Now, Gillman again, you do not know the treasure of the Fullers. I calculate on having massy reading till Christmas. All I want here is books of the true sort, not those things in 10 boards that moderns mistake for books—what they club for at book clubs.

To Bernard Barton.

December 8, 1829.

I write big not to save ink but eyes, mine having been troubled with reading thro' three folios of old Fuller in almost as few days, and I went to bed last night in agony, and am writing with a vial of eye-water before me, alternately dipping in vial and inkstand. . . .

Wishing you and yours all Health, I conclude while these frail glasses are to me—eyes.   C. L.   20

are supposed to have been incapable of nature or feeling : they are usually opposed to such writers as Shenstone and Parnel ; whereas in the very thickest of their conceits,—in the bewildering maze of their tropes and figures, a warmth of soul and generous feeling shines through, the ' sum ' of which, ' forty thousand ' of those natural poets, as they are called, ' with all their quantity, could not make up.'—Without any intention of setting Fuller on a level with Donne or Cowley, I think the injustice which has been done him in the denial that he possesses any other qualities than those of a quaint and conceited writer, is of the same kind as that with which these two great Poets have been treated. 1811.]

To James Gillman.

1830.

DEAR GILLMAN,—Pray do you or S. T. C. immediately write to say you have received back the golden works of the dear, fine, silly old angel, which I part from, bleeding, and to say how the Winter has used you all. . . .

Yours, mopish, but in health,

C. LAMB.

I shall be uneasy till I hear of Fuller's safe arrival.

JAMES CROSSLEY on FULLER

(The Retrospective Review, vol. iii, 1821)

HE absolutely communicates something of his own fervour to his reader : it is almost impossible to read his works without going along with him in his hunt for jokes, and without participating in his satisfaction when he has found them. His quaint facetiousness was communicable to every thing. Graft it on whatever tree he chose, and it would bud out, blossom forth, and luxuriate. Like a fisherman, he threw out his capacious net into the ocean of wit, and rejected nothing that it brought up, however miscellaneous or motley were its contents ; pleased, and perhaps thinking that others would be pleased, with their variety. There is besides such an apparent self-satisfaction discernible throughout his works—we can almost fancy we see him chuckling over his forth-coming jests as they successively issue from his brain, preparing us by his triumphant exulta- tion for the stroke which is to follow : or revelling in un- controled and uncontrolable merriment over the vagaries of which he had discharged his head by communicating them to paper. Such was the disposition of Fuller. The qualities of mind which would in another have produced a buffoon, in him, without losing their power of entertainment, lost all their grosser and more offensive traits, and became, from their very superfetation, less imbued with the rankness of farce. To him the language of jocularity had something of the gravity of earnest : it was his own vernacular idiom, in which every thing which issued from his mind was clothed ; it was something so intimately connected with him, that all attempts to strip it off would be useless ; something settled and fixed in his intellect, and stamping and marking its whole character. By being therefore more generalized, it had less of marked purport and design, and as it was assumed on all subjects was indecorous on none.— Fuller, we think, would hardly have scrupled to crack a joke upon the four Evangelists ; but certain we are, it would have been without any idea of indecency or intention of irreverence.

This characteristic peculiarity is equally visible in all his productions, from his *Holy War* to his *Worthies*, and consequently they are all almost equally entertaining. His *Holy War* and *Church History*, particularly the last, are two of the most agreeable works we know ; replete, besides their Fullerism, with perspicacious observation, profound thought, deep discernment, and narrative power. There are specimens of historical painting in these works which perhaps have never been excelled, conceived with great energy and executed with happiness.—In his delineation of characters, he exhibits such unrivalled acumen, ability, and penetration, together with such candour and uprightness of judgment, that it is difficult which most to admire, his sagacity or his sincerity. His *Pisgah Sight of Palestine*, which is also in part an historical work, is a happy elucidation of what Fuller always excelled in, sacred story : and no work of his better displays the riches of his mind or the plenitude and fertility of its images. His *Worthies* is, we

believe, more generally perused than any of his productions, and is perhaps the most agreeable ; suffice to say of it, that it is a most fascinating storehouse of gossiping, anecdote, and quaintness ; a most delightful medley of interchanged amusement, presenting entertainment as varied as it is inexhaustible. His *Good Thoughts in Bad Times*, and lesser works, are all equally excellent in their way, full of admirable maxims and reflections, agreeable stories, and ingenious moralizations. It was however in biography that
10 Fuller most excelled.—If he was frequently too careless and inaccurate in his facts, it was not from heedlessness as to truth, which no one reverenced more than he did, but because he considered them but as the rind and outward covering of the more important and more delicious stores of thinking and consideration which they inwardly contained ; because he thought life too short to be frittered away in fixing dates and examining registers : what he sought was matter convertible to use, to the great work of the improvement of the human mind, not those more minute
20 and jejune creatures of authenticity, which fools toil in seeking after, and madmen die in elucidating. In this he has been followed by a great biographical writer of the last age, with whom he had more points than one in common. Leaving therefore such minor parts of biography for the investigation of others, and seizing only on the principal events, and those distinguishing incidents or anecdotes which mark a character in a moment, and which no one knew better than Fuller to pick out and select, he detailed them with such perspicuity and precision, and commented upon them with
30 such accuracy of discrimination, strength of argument and force of reason, and threw around them such a luminous and lambent halo of sparkling quaintness, shining upon and playing about the matter of his thoughts, and inspirited them with such omnipresent jocularity and humour, that,

of all the biographical writers of his age, he is, in our opinion, infinitely the best. After the perusal of the more polished, but certainly not more agreeable biographers of modern times, we always recur with renewed gusto and avidity to the Lives of our excellent author, as to a feast more substantial, without being less delicious.

LESLIE STEPHEN on FULLER

(*The Cornhill Magazine*, January 1872)

THE peculiarity of Fuller is not that he makes far-fetched quotations, or that his logical gambols are of the most unaccountable nature. So far he is merely adopting a recognized method in which half the preachers and writers of his time might be his rivals. His merit is that his most fantastic caprices are always witty. Nothing is more wearisome than this incessant straining of the invention in the hands of an essentially dull writer ; the jokes of such a man are always missing fire. Fuller's instinct is infallible ; he touches his queer fancies so lightly that you are never disgusted ; if for a moment he seems to be serious, he is instantly off upon some outrageous conceit which would extort laughter from a bishop at a funeral. . . .

It is comparatively rare for Fuller to rise to the borders of that lofty region of eloquence where Sir Thomas Browne treads like a native. In fact, he is little given to soaring, and distinctly prefers the earth to the clouds ; his wisdom is such as comes from excellent good sense, without any great profundity of thought ; his piety is that of a cheerful and admirably expressive person who has never sounded the depths of despair or risen to ecstatic rapture ; and his wit owes its charm to its being obviously the spontaneous outburst of a nature of irrepressible buoyancy and childlike frivolity of amusement.   Whatever emotion is excited in his breast, it seems to stir him to the same outward expression. . . .

Amusing as is Fuller's narrative style, he seems to me to be still better in his didactic humour.   He is great at a sententious moral aphorism ; and comments on the aphorism, ludicrous or serious, really illustrative or utterly irrelevant, fairly jostle each other in their haste for expression.   In his most popular book, the *Holy and Profane State*, brief essays and descriptions of typical characters are mixed up with biographies intended to exemplify the didactic matter.   Wit and wisdom, shrewd observation, and kindly feeling are spread through its pages in profusion.   Perhaps the best measure of its merits may be obtained by comparing it with the performance of another great master of English, though in a different style.   Some of Bacon's essays deal with the same topics, and the contrast is instructive.   Fuller, for example, and Bacon have both something to say upon the well-worn topic of marriage.   As marriage has been discussed by innumerable sages and satirists, from the days of Solomon to those of the *Saturday Review*, we cannot expect any positively new lights from our authors.   There is, however, no better test of high literary skill than the power of making the proposition that two and two make four sound like a new and startling truth.   Both writers succeed in giving interest to a subject where the only choice appears to lie between truisms and paradoxes, but by curiously different devices.   More than one of Bacon's weighty sentences have passed into proverbs.   ' He that hath a wife and children hath given hostages unto fortune,' ' Wives are young men's mistresses, the companions of middle-age, and old men's nurses.'   Bacon's sentences are heavy with thought, as though compressed in a kind of intellectual hydraulic machine.   Like Lord Thurlow, they look wiser than any sentence ever really was. Now, take Fuller's treatment of a thought identical with one of Bacon's : ' Though bachelors be the strongest stakes ', he says, ' married men are the best binders in the hedge of the commonwealth.' ' . . . Married men, especially if having posterity, are the deeper sharers in that state wherein they live, which engageth their affections to the greater loyalty.' This last sentence reads like a clumsy paraphrase of Bacon's aphorism ; the metaphor, though rather odd, is perhaps less strained than most of Fuller's. But he soon makes amends. We are not, he says, to expect too much from matrimony ; and this text is embroidered as follows : ' Marriage is not like the hill Olympus—ὅλος λαμπρός—*wholly clear*, without clouds ; you expect both wind and storms sometimes, which, when blown over, the air is the clearer and wholesomer for it. Make account of certain cares and troubles which will attend thee. Remember the nightingales, which sing only some months in spring, but commonly are silent when they have hatched their eggs, as if their mirth were turned into care for their young ones.' The illustration is pretty and fanciful, and he gives us half-a-dozen more in the next page. Bacon only indulges in one metaphor, but that is one which is an argument instead of a mere ornament. ' A single life ', he says, ' doth well with churchmen ; for charity will hardly water the ground where it must first fill a pool.' Bacon's sententious gravity raises a common-place to the rank of a grand philosophical axiom ; Fuller's discursive fancy invests it with all the airs of a startling paradox. . . .

In Bacon's essays there is always that sub-acid flavour natural to a man who has had harsh experience and looked at the seamy side of things as well as their surface. Fuller always shows the almost provoking optimism engendered by an easy and prosperous life, whilst even his subsequent trials never seem to have soured him. Both writers, for

example, remark that the king ' is a mortal god ' : but Bacon characteristically adds, ' of all kinds of men God is the least beholden unto them ; for he doth most for them, and they do ordinarily least for him.' Both are eloquent on the advantage of combining justice and mercy. Fuller, after some characteristic remarks, concludes that ' in his mercy our king (that is, the ideal king) desires to resemble the God of heaven, who measureth his judgments by the ordinary cubit, but his kindnesses by the cubit of the sanctuary—twice as big '. Bacon, on the other hand, observes, ' that the restraint of justice towards sin doth more retard the affection of love than the extent of mercy doth inflame it '. Bacon speaks of kings and criminals like a shrewd lawyer and statesman ; Fuller like a good-humoured country clergyman, who expects everybody to be as good and happy as himself. In fact, when we endeavour to sum up Fuller's character, that is, perhaps, the last impression that remains with us. His simplicity is certainly not unmingled with a certain shrewdness, of which the following remark, as appropriate to the present day, may be a sufficient instance : ' Charity mistaken, which relieves idle people, like a dead corpse, only feeds the vermin it breeds ' ; but we feel certain that if Fuller met an idle beggar after writing that sentence, he relieved him with the most utter disregard of sound economical doctrines. Some such case was in his mind when in his *Good Thoughts* he ponders over the problem whether he is responsible for the crimes that were committed by a villain whom he had saved from starvation on the promise of reform, and who, as usual, forgot his promise.
Fuller's remorse for a good-natured action was not, we may be sure, very deep. In fact, we may doubt whether he ever could know what melancholy meant. When his party was on the road to ruin, he wrote *Good Thoughts in Bad Times* ; when it was ruined, he wrote *Good Thoughts in Worse Times* ;

and when it was rising from the ground, *Mixed Contemplations in Better Times*. And the remarkable circumstance is
that all his thoughts are as cheerful as anybody else would
have in the best of times. No misfortune could damp his
spirits or diminish his intense affection for a pun. He was
the most buoyant of mankind ; and if he ever knew what
it was to be melancholy, he could find relief in lamentations
so lively as to sound like an effusion of exuberant spirits.
The wonder is that we feel this boyish exhilaration to be
significant of true feeling. Some men shed tears when they 10
are deeply moved ; Fuller pours forth a string of quibbles.
It is a singular idiosyncrasy which inverts the conventional
modes of expressing devotion, and makes jokes, good, bad,
and indifferent, do duty for sighs. But nobody should read
Fuller who cannot more or less understand the frame of
mind to which such fantastic freaks are congenial ; and
those who do will learn that, if in one sense he is the most
childlike, in another he is amongst the most manly of writers.
He enjoys a sort of rude intellectual health, which enables
him to relish childish amusements to the end of his days ; 20
and it is difficult to imagine a more enviable accomplish-
ment, though it must be admitted that it leads to some
rather startling literary phenomena.

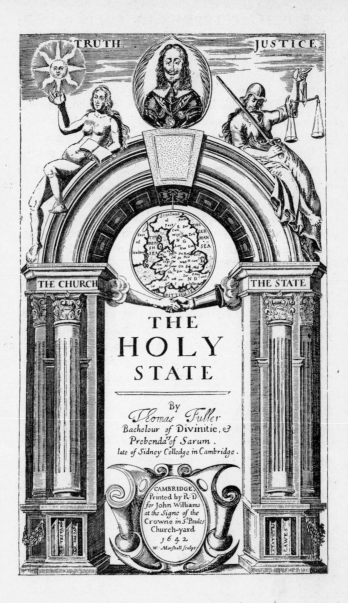

TRUTH

JUSTICE.

THE CHURCH

THE STATE

THE
HOLY
STATE

By
Thomas Fuller
Bachelour of Divinitie, &
Prebenda.ᵣ of Sarum .
late of Sidney Colledge in Cambridge .

CAMBRIDGE,
Printed by R. D
for John Williams
at the Signe of the
Crowne in Sᵗ Paules
Church-yard
1642
W. Marshall sculpt

THE HOLY STATE

To the Reader

WHO is not sensible with sorrow of the distractions of this age ? To write books therefore may seem unseasonable, especially in a time wherein the *Presse*, like an unruly horse, hath cast off his bridle of being *Licensed*, and some serious books, which dare flie abroad, are hooted at by a flock of Pamphlets.

But be pleased to know that when I left my home, it was fair weather, and my journey was half past, before I discovered the tempest, and had gone so farre in this Work, that I could neither go backward with credit, nor forward with comfort.

As for the matter of this Book, therein I am resident on my Profession ; Holinesse in the latitude thereof falling under the cognizanse of a Divine. For curious method, expect none, Essays for the most part not being placed as at a *Feast*, but placing themselves as at an *Ordinary*.

The characters I have conformed to the then standing Laws of the Realm, (a twelvemoneth agoe were they sent to the presse) since which time the wisdome of the King and State hath thought fitting to alter many things, and I expect the discretion of the Reader should make his alterations accordingly. And I conjure thee by all Christian ingenuity, that if lighting here on some passages, rather harsh-sounding then ill-intended, to construe the same by the generall drift and main scope which is aimed at.

Nor let it render the modestie of this Book suspected, because it presumes to appear in company unmann'd by any Patron : If right, it will defend it self ; if wrong, none can defend it : Truth needs not, falshood deserves not a

Supporter. And indeed the matter of this Work is too high for a subjects, the workmanship thereof too low for a Princes patronage.

And now I will turn my pen into prayer, That God would be pleased to discloud these gloomy dayes with the beams of his mercie : which if I may be so happy as to see, it will then encourage me to count it freedome to serve two apprentiships (God spinning out the thick thred of my life so long) in writing the Ecclesiastical History from Christs time to our dayes, if I shall from remoter parts be so planted, as to enjoy the benefit of walking, and standing Libraries, without which advantages the best vigilancie doth but vainly dream to undertake such a task.

Mean time I will stop the leakage of my soul, and what heretofore hath run out in writing, shall hereafter (God willing) be improved in constant preaching, in what place soever Gods providence, and friends good will shall fix

Thine in all Christian offices

THOMAS FULLER.

The generall Artist

I KNOW the generall cavill against generall learning is this, that *aliquis in omnibus est nullus in singulis.* He that sips of many arts, drinks of none. However we must know, that all learning, which is but one grand Science, hath so homogeneall a body, that the parts thereof do with a mutuall service relate to, and communicate strength and lustre each to other. Our Artist knowing language to be the key of learning, thus begins.

His tongue being but one by nature he gets cloven by art and industry. Before the confusion of Babel, all the world was one continent in language ; since divided into severall tongues, as severall ilands. Grammer is the ship, by benefit whereof we passe from one to another, in the learned languages generally spoken in no countrey. His mothertongue was like the dull musick of a monochord, which by study he turns into the harmony of severall instruments.

He first gaineth skill in the Latine and Greek tongues. On the credit of the former alone, he may trade in discourse over all Christendome : But the Greek, though not so generally spoken, is known with no lesse profit, and more pleasure. The joynts of her compounded words are so naturally oyled, that they run nimbly on the tongue ; which makes them though long never tedious, because significant. Besides, it is full and stately in sound : onely it pities our Artist to see the vowels therein rackt in pronouncing them, hanging oftentimes one way by their native force, and haled another by their accents which countermand them.

Hence he proceeds to the Hebrew, the mother-tongue of the world. More pains then quicknesse of wit is required to get it, and with daily exercise he continues it. Apostacy herein is usuall to fall totally from the language by a little neglect. As for the Arabick, and other Orientall languages, he rather makes sallies and incursions into them, then any solemn sitting down before them.

Then he applies his study to Logick, and Ethicks. The latter makes a mans soul mannerly and wise ; but as for Logick, that is the armory of reason, furnished with all offensive and defensive weapons. There are Syllogismes, long swords ; Enthymems, short daggers ; Dilemma's, two-edged swords that cut on both sides ; Sorites, chain-shot : And for the defensive, Distinctions, which are shields ; Retortions, which are targets with a pike in the midst of them, both to defend and oppose. From hence he raiseth his studies to the knowledge of Physicks, the great hall of Nature, and Metaphysicks the closet thereof ; and is carefull

not to wade therein so farre, till by subtle distinguishing
of notions he confounds himself.

*He is skilfull in Rhetorick, which gives a speech colour, as
Logick doth favour, and both together beauty.* Though some
condemne Rhetorick as the mother of lies, speaking more
then the truth in Hyperboles, lesse in her Miosis, otherwise
in her metaphors, contrary in her ironies ; yet is there
excellent use of all these, when disposed of with judgement.
Nor is he a stranger to Poetry, which is musick in words ;
nor to Musick, which is poetry in sound : both excellent
sauce, but they have liv'd and died poore, that made them
their meat.

*Mathematicks he moderately studieth to his great content-
ment.* Using it as ballast for his soul, yet to fix it not to stall
it ; nor suffers he it to be so unmannerly as to justle out
other arts. As for judiciall Astrology (which hath the least
judgement in it) this vagrant hath been whipt out of all
learned corporations. If our Artist lodgeth her in the out-
rooms of his soul for a night or two, it is rather to heare
then believe her relations.

Hence he makes his progresse into the study of History.
Nestor, who lived three ages, was accounted the wisest man
in the world. But the Historian may make himself wise
by living as many ages as have past since the beginning of
the world. His books enable him to maintain discourse,
who besides the stock of his own experience may spend on
the common purse of his reading. This directs him in his
life, so that he makes the shipwracks of others sea-marks to
himself ; yea accidents which others start from for their
strangenes, he welcomes as his wonted acquaintance, having
found presidents for them formerly. Without History a
mans soul is purblind, seeing onely the things which almost
touch his eyes.

He is well seen in Chronology, without which History is but an heap of tales. If by the Laws of the land he is counted a Naturall, who hath not wit enough to tell twenty, or to tell his age ; he shall not passe with me for wise in learning, who cannot tell the age of the world, and count hundreds of years : I mean not so critically, as to solve all doubts arising thence ; but that he may be able to give some tolerable account thereof. He is also acquainted with Cosmography, treating of the world in whole joynts ; with Chorography, shredding it into countries ; and with Topography, mincing it into particular places.   10

Thus taking these Sciences in their generall latitude, he hath finished the round circle or golden ring of the arts ; onely he keeps a place for the diamond to be set in, I mean for that predominant profession of Law, Physick, Divinity, or State-policie, which he intends for his principall Calling hereafter.

                                                (Book II, Chap. 7)

The good Yeoman

Is a Gentleman in Ore, whom the next age may see refined ; and is the wax capable of a gentile impression, when the Prince shall stamp it. Wise Solon (who accounted Tellus the Athenian the most happy man for living privately 20 on his own lands) would surely have pronounced the English Yeomanry, a fortunate condition, living in the temperate Zone, betwixt greatnesse and want, an estate of people almost peculiar to England. France and Italy are like a die, which hath no points betwixt sink and ace, Nobility and Pesantry. Their walls though high, must needs be hollow, wanting filling-stones. Indeed Germany hath her Boores, like our Yeomen, but by a tyrannicall appropriation of Nobility to some few ancient families, their Yeomen are excluded from ever rising higher to clarifie their bloods. In 30 England the Temple of Honour is bolted against none, who

have passed through the Temple of Virtue : nor is a capacity
to be gentile denyed to our Yeoman, who thus behaves
himself.

He wears russet clothes, but makes golden payment, having
tinne in his buttons, and silver in his pocket. If he chance
to appear in clothes above this rank, it is to grace some
great man with his service, and then he blusheth at his
own bravery. Otherwise he is the surest landmark, whence
forreiners may take aim of the ancient English customes ;
10 the Gentry more floting after forrein fashions.

*In his house he is bountifull both to strangers, and poore
people.* Some hold, when Hospitality dyed in England, she
gave her last groan amongst the Yeomen of Kent. And still
at our Yeomans table you shall have as many joints as
dishes : No meat disguis'd with strange sauces ; no strag-
gling joynt of a sheep in the midst of a pasture of grasse,
beset with sallads on every side, but solid substantiall food ;
no serviters (more nimble with their hands then the guests
with their teeth) take away meat, before stomachs are taken
20 away. Here you have that which in it self is good, made
better by the store of it, and best by the welcome to it.

He hath a great stroke in making a Knight of the shire.
Good reason, for he makes a whole line in the subsidie-book,
where whatsoever he is rated he payes without any regret,
not caring how much his purse is let blood, so it be done by
the advise of the physicians of the State.

*He seldome goes farre abroad, and his credit stretcheth
further then his travell.* He goes not to London, but *se de-
fendendo,* to save himself of a fine, being returned of a Jurie,
30 where seeing the King once, he prayes for him ever afterwards.

In his own countrey he is a main man in Juries. Where if
the Judge please to open his eyes in matter of law, he needs
not to be led by the nose in matters of fact. He is very

observant of the Judges *item*, when it follows the truths *inprimis* ; otherwise (though not mutinous in a Jurie) he cares not whom he displeaseth so he pleaseth his own conscience.

He improveth his land to a double value by his good husbandry. Some grounds that wept with water, or frown'd with thorns, by draining the one, and clearing the other, he makes both to laugh and sing with corn. By marle and limestones burnt he bettereth his ground, and his industry worketh miracles, by turning stones into bread. Conquest and good husbandry both inlarge the Kings Dominions : The one by the sword, making the acres more in number ; the other by the plough, making the same acres more in value. Solomon saith, *The King himself is maintained by husbandry.* Pythis a King having discovered rich mines in his kingdome, employed all his people in digging of them, whence tilling was wholly neglected, insomuch as a great famine ensued. His Queen, sensible of the calamities of the countrey, invited the King her husband to dinner, as he came home hungry from overseeing his workmen in the mines. She so contrived it, that the bread and meat were most artificially made of gold ; and the King was much delighted with the conceit thereof, till at last he called for reall meat to satisfie his hunger. *Nay,* said the Queen, *if you employ all your subjects in your mines, you must expect to feed upon gold, for nothing else can your kingdome afford.*

In time of famine he is the Joseph of the countrey, and keeps the poore from sterving. Then he tameth his stacks of corn, which not his covetousnesse but providence hath reserv'd for time of need, and to his poore neighbours abateth somewhat of the high price of the market. The neighbour gentry court him for his acquaintance, which he either modestly waveth, or thankfully accepteth, but no way greedily desireth. He insults not on the ruines of a decayed Gentleman, but pities and relieves him : and as he is called *Good-man*, he desires to answer to the name, and to be so indeed.

In warre, though he serveth on foot, he is ever mounted on an high spirit : as being a slave to none, and a subject onely to his own Prince. Innocence and independance make a brave spirit : Whereas otherwise one must ask his leave to be valiant on whom he depends. Therefore if a State run up all to Noblemen and Gentlemen, so that the husbandmen be onely mere labourers, or cottagers, (which one calls but

10 hous'd beggers) it may have good Cavalry, but never good bands of foot ; so that their armies will be like those birds call'd *Apodes*, without feet, alwayes onely flying on their wings of horse. Wherefore to make good Infantry, it requir-eth men bred, not in a servile or indigent fashion, but in some free and plentifull manner. Wisely therefore did that knowing Prince, King Henry the seventh, provide laws for the increase of his Yeomanry, that his kingdome should not be like to Coppice-woods, where the staddles being left too thick, all runs to bushes and briers, and there 's little clean

20 underwood. For enacting, that houses used to husbandry should be kept up with a competent proportion of land, he did secretly sow Hydra's teeth, whereupon (according to the Poets fiction) should rise up armed men for the service of this kingdome.

(Book II, Chap. 18)

The good Sea-Captain

HIS Military part is concurrent with that of the Souldier already described : He differs onely in some Sea-properties, which we will now set down. Conceive him now in a Man of warre, with his letters of mart, well arm'd victuall'd and appointed, and see how he acquits himself.

30 *The more power he hath, the more carefull he is not to abuse*

it. Indeed a Sea-captain is a King in the Iland of a ship, supreme Judge, above appeal, in causes civill and criminall, and is seldome brought to an account in Courts of Justice on land, for injuries done to his own men at sea.

He is carefull in observing of the Lords day. He hath a watch in his heart though no bells in a steeple to proclaim that day by ringing to prayers. Sr. Francis Drake in three years sailing about the world lost one whole day, which was scarce considerable in so long time. 'Tis to be feared some Captains at sea lose a day every week, one in seven, neglecting the Sabbath.

He is as pious and thankfull when a tempest is past, as devout when 'tis present : not clamorous to receive mercies, and tongue-tied to return thanks. Many mariners are calm in a storm, and storm in a calm, blustring with oathes. In a tempest it comes to their turn to be religious, whose piety is but a fit of the wind, and when that's allayed, their devotion is ended.

Escaping many dangers makes him not presumptuous to run into them. Not like those Sea-men who (as if their hearts were made of those rocks they have often sayled by) are so alwayes in death they never think of it. These in their navigations observe that it is farre hotter under the Tropicks in the coming to the Line, then under the Line it self, and in like manner they conceive that the fear and phancy in preparing for death is more terrible then death it self, which makes them by degrees desperately to contemne it.

In taking a prize he most prizeth the mens lives whom he takes ; though some of them may chance to be Negroes or Savages. 'Tis the custome of some to cast them overbord, and there's an end of them : for the dumbe fishes will tell no tales. But the murder is not so soon drown'd as the men. What, is a brother by the half bloud no kinne ? a Savage hath God to his father by creation, though not the Church to his mother, and God will revenge his innocent bloud. But our Captain counts the image of God neverthelesse his image cut in ebony as if done in ivory, and in the blackest Moores he sees the representation of the King of heaven.

In dividing the gains he wrongs none who took pains to get them. Not shifting off his poore mariners with nothing, or giving them onely the garbage of the prize, and keeping all the flesh to himself. In time of peace he quietly returns home, and turns not to the trade of Pirates, who are the
10 worst sea-vermine, and the devils water-rats.

His voyages are not onely for profit, but some for honour and knowledge ; to make discoveries of new countreys, imitating the worthy Peter Columbus. Before his time the world was cut off at the middle ; Hercules Pillars (which indeed are the navell) being made the feet, and utmost bounds of the continent, till his successefull industry inlarged it.

> *Primus ab infusis quod terra emerserat undis*
> *Nuncius adveniens ipsa Columba fuit.*
> *Occiduis primus qui terram invenit in undis*
20 *Nuncius adveniens ipse Columbus erat.*

Our Sea-captain is likewise ambitious to perfect what the other began. He counts it a disgrace, seeing all mankind is one familie, sundry countreys but severall rooms, that we who dwell in the parlour (so he counts Europe) should not know the out-lodgings of the same house, and the world be scarce acquainted with it self before it be dissolved from it self at the day of judgement.

He daily sees, and duly considers Gods wonders in the deep. Tell me, ye Naturalists, who sounded the first march and
30 retreat to the Tide, *Hither shalt thou come, and no further ?* why doth not the water recover his right over the earth, being higher in nature ? whence came the salt, and who first boyled it, which made so much brine ? when the winds are not onely wild in a storm, but even stark mad in an

herricano, who is it that restores them again to their wits, and brings them asleep in a calm ? who made the mighty whales, who swim in a sea of water, and have a sea of oyl swimming in them ? who first taught the water to imitate the creatures on land ? so that the sea is the stable of horse-fishes, the stall of kine-fishes, the stye of hog-fishes, the kennell of dog-fishes, and in all things the sea the ape of the land. Whence growes the amber-greece in the Sea ? which is not so hard to find where it is, as to know what it is. Was not God the first shipwright ? and all vessels on the water descended from the loyns (or ribs rather) of Noahs ark ; or else who durst be so bold with a few crooked boards nayled together, a stick standing upright, and a rag tied to it, to adventure into the ocean ? what loadstone first touched the loadstone ? or how first fell it in love with the North, rather affecting that cold climate, then the pleasant East, or fruitfull South, or West ? how comes that stone to know more then men, and find the way to the land in a mist ? In most of these men take sanctuary at *Occulta qualitas*, and complain that the room is dark, when their eyes are blind. Indeed they are Gods Wonders ; and that Seaman the greatest Wonder of all for his blockishnesse, who seeing them dayly neither takes notice of them, admires at them, nor is thankfull for them.

(Book II, Chap. 20)

The life of Sir Francis Drake

FRANCIS DRAKE was born nigh south Tavestock in Devon-shire, and brought up in Kent ; God dividing the honour betwixt two Counties, that the one might have his birth, and the other his education. His Father, being a Minister, fled into Kent for fear of the Six Articles, wherein the sting of Popery still remained in England, though the teeth thereof were knock'd out, and the Popes Supremacy abolished. Coming into Kent, he bound his sonne Francis apprentice to the Master of a small bark, which traded into France, and Zealand, where he underwent a hard service ; and pains with patience in his youth did knit the joynts of his soul, and made them more solid and compacted. His Master dying unmarried, in reward of his industry, bequeath'd his bark unto him for a Legacie.

For some time he continued his Masters profession : But the Narrow Seas were a prison for so large a spirit, born for greater undertakings. He soon grew weary of his bark, which would scarce go alone but as it crept along by the shore : wherefore selling it, he unfortunately ventured most of his estate with Captain John Hawkins into the West Indies, whose goods were taken by the Spaniards at S. John de Ulva, and he himself scarce escaped with life. The King of Spain being so tender in those parts, that the least touch doth wound him ; and so jealous of the West Indies, his wife, that willingly he would have none look upon her, and therefore used them with the greater severity.

Drake was perswaded by the Minister of his ship that he might lawfully recover in value of the King of Spain, and repair his losses upon him any where else. The Case was clear in sea-divinity, and few are such Infidels, as not to believe doctrines which make for their own profit. Whereupon Drake, though a poore private man, hereafter undertook to revenge himself on so mighty a Monarch ; who, as not contented that the Sun riseth and setteth in his dominions, may seem to desire to make all his own where he shineth. And now let us see how a dwarf, standing on the Mount of Gods providence, may prove an overmatch for a giant.

After two or three severall Voyages to gain intelligence in the West Indies, and some prizes taken, at last he effectually set forward from Plimouth with two ships, the one of seventy, the other twenty five tunnes, and seventy three men and boyes in both. He made with all speed and secrecy to Nombre de Dios, as loth to put the Town to too much charge (which he knew they would willingly bestow) in providing beforehand for his entertainment ; which City was then the granary of the West Indies, wherein the golden harvest brought from Panama was hoarded up till it could be conveyed into Spain. They came hard aboard the shore, and lay quiet all night intending to attempt the Town in 10 the dawning of the day.

But he was forced to alter his resolution, and assault it sooner ; for he heard his men muttering amongst themselves of the strength and greatnesse of the Town : and when mens heads are once fly-blown with buzzes of suspicion, the vermine multiply instantly, and one jealousie begets another. Wherefore he raised them from their nest before they had hatch'd their fears, and to put away those conceits, he perswaded them it was day-dawning when the Moon rose, and instantly set on the Town, and wonne it being 20 unwalled. In the Market-place the Spaniards saluted them with a volley of shot ; Drake returned their greeting with a flight of arrows, the best and ancient English complement, which drave their enemies away. Here Drake received a dangerous wound, though he valiantly conceal'd it a long time, knowing if his heart stooped, his mens would fall, and loth to leave off the action, wherein if so bright an opportunity once setteth, it seldome riseth again. But at length his men forced him to return to his ship, that his wound might be dressed, and this unhappy accident defeated the 30 whole designe. Thus victory sometimes slips thorow their fingers, who have caught it in their hands.

But his valour would not let him give over the project as long as there was either life or warmth in it : And therefore having received intelligence from the Negroes, called Symerons, of many mules-lading of gold and silver, which was to be brought from Panama, he leaving competent numbers to man his ships went on land with the rest, and bestowed himself in the woods by the way as they were to passe, and so intercepted and carried away an infinite masse of gold. As for the silver which was not portable over the mountains, they digged holes in the ground and hid it therein.

10   There want not those who love to beat down the price of every honourable action, though they themselves never mean to be chapmen. These cry up Drakes fortune herein to cry down his valour ; as if this his performance were nothing, wherein a golden opportunity ran his head with his long forelock into Drakes hands beyond expectation. But certainly his resolution and unconquerable patience deserved much praise, to adventure on such a designe, which had in it just no more probability then what was enough to keep it from being impossible : yet I admire not so much at all 20 the treasure he took, as at the rich and deep mine of Gods providence.

Having now full fraughted himself with wealth, and burnt at the House of Crosses above two hundred thousand pounds worth of Spanish Merchandise, he returned with honour and safety into England, and some years after undertook that his famous voyage about the world, most accurately described by our English Authours : and yet a word or two thereof will not be amisse.

Setting forward from Plimouth, he bore up for Caboverd, 30 where near to the Iland of S. Jago he took prisoner Nuno-da-Silva, an experienc'd Spanish pilot, whose direction he used in the coasts of Brasil and Magellan straits, and afterwards safely landed him at Guatulco in New Spain. Hence they took their course to the iland of Brava, and hereabouts

they met with those tempestuous winds, whose onely praise
is, that they continue not above an houre, in which time
they change all the points of the compasse. Here they had
great plenty of rain, poured (not as in other places, as it
were out of sives, but) as out of spouts, so that a but of
water falls down in a place : which notwithstanding is but
a courteous injury in that hot climate farre from land, and
where otherwise fresh water cannot be provided : then
cutting the Line, they saw the face of that heaven which
earth hideth from us, but therein onely three starres of the 10
first greatnesse, the rest few and small compared to our
Hemisphere, as if God, on purpose, had set up the best and
biggest candles in that room wherein his civilest guests are
entertained.

Sayling the South of Brasile, he afterwards passed the
Magellan straits, and then entred *Mare pacificum*, came to
the Southernmost land at the height of $55\frac{1}{2}$ latitude ; thence
directing his course Northward, he pillaged many Spanish
Towns, and took rich prizes of high value in the kingdomes
of Chily, Peru, and New Spain. Then bending Eastwards, 20
he coasted China, and the Moluccoes, where by the King
of Terrenate, a true Gentleman Pagan, he was most honourably entertain'd : The King told them, They and he were
all of one religion in this respect, that they believed not
in Gods made of stocks and stones as did the Portugalls.
He furnish'd them also with all necessaries that they wanted.

On the ninth of January following, his ship, having a
large wind and a smooth sea, ran a ground on a dangerous
shole, and strook twice on it, knocking twice at the doore
of death, which no doubt had opened the third time. Here 30
they stuck from eight a clock at night till foure the next
afternoon, having ground too much, and yet too little to
land on, and water too much, and yet too little to sail in.
Had God (*who*, as the wiseman saith, Prov. 30. 4. *holdeth*

the winds in his fist) but opened his little finger, and let out the smallest blast, they had undoubtedly been cast away; but there blew not any wind all the while. Then they conceiving aright that the best way to lighten the ship, was first to ease it of the burthen of their sinnes by true repentance, humbled themselves by fasting under the hand of God: Afterwards they received the Communion, dining on Christ in the Sacrament, expecting no other then to sup with him in heaven: Then they cast out of their ship six great pieces of ordinance, threw over-board as much wealth as would break the heart of a Miser to think on't, with much suger, and packs of spices, making a caudle of the sea round about: Then they betook themselves to their prayers, the best lever at such a dead lift indeed, and it pleased God that the wind, formerly their mortall enemy, became their friend, which changing from the Starboard to the Larboard of the ship, and rising by degrees, cleared them off to the sea again, for which they returned unfeigned thanks to almighty God.

By the Cape of good hope and west of Africa he returned safe into England, and landed at Plimouth, (being almost the first of those that made a thorow-light through the world) having in his whole voyage, though a curious searcher after the time, lost one day through the variation of severall Climates. He feasted the Queen in his ship at Dartford, who Knighted him for his service: yet it grieved him not a little, that some prime Courtiers refused the gold he offer'd them, as gotten by piracy. Some of them would have been loth to have been told, that they had *Aurum Tholosanum* in their own purses. Some think that they did it to shew that their envious pride was above their covetousnesse, who of set purpose did blur the fair copy of his performance, because they would not take pains to write after it.

I passe by his next West Indian voyage, wherein he took the Cities of S. Jago, S. Domingo, Carthagena, and S.

Augustine in Florida : as also his service performed in 88, wherein he with many others helped to the waining of that half Moon, which sought to govern all the motion of our Sea. I hast to his last Voyage.

Queen Elizabeth perceiving that the onely way to make the Spaniard a criple for ever, was to cut his Sinews of warre in the West Indies, furnished Sr. Francis Drake, and Sr. John Hawkins with six of her own ships, besides 21 ships and Barks of their own providing, containing in all 2500 Men and Boyes, for some service on America. But, alas, this voyage was marr'd before begun. For so great preparations being too big for a cover, the King of Spain knew of it, and sent a Caravall of adviso to the West Indies, so that they had intelligence three weeks before the Fleet set forth of England, either to fortifie, or remove their treasure ; whereas in other of Drakes Voyages not two of his own men knew whither he went ; and managing such a designe is like carrying a Mine in warre, if it hath any vent, all is spoyled. Besides, Drake and Hawkins being in joynt Commission hindred each other. The later took himself to be inferiour rather in successe then skill, and the action was unlike to prosper when neither would follow, and both could not handsomly go abreast. It vexed old Hawkins that his counsell was not followed, in present sayling to America, but that they spent time in vain in assaulting the Canaries ; and the grief that his advice was slighted (say some) was the cause of his death. Others impute it to the sorrow he took, for the taking of his Bark called the Francis, which five Spanish Frigates had intercepted : But when the same heart hath two mortall wounds given it together, 'tis hard to say which of them killeth.

Drake continued his course for Port-Rico, and riding within the roade, a shot from the Castle entred the steerage of the ship, took away the stool from under him as he sate at supper, wounded Sr. Nicholas Clifford and Brute Brown to death. *Ah dear Brute* (said Drake) *I could grieve for thee, but now is no time for me to let down my spirits.* And indeed a Souldiers most proper bemoaning a friends death in warre is in revenging it. And sure, as if grief had made the English furious, they soon after fired five Spanish ships of two hundred tunnes apiece, in despight of the Castle.

America is not unfitly resembled to an Houre-glasse, which hath a narrow neck of land (suppose it the hole where the sand passeth) betwixt the parts thereof, Mexicana and Pervana. Now the English had a designe to march by land over this Isthmus from Port-Rico to Panama, where the Spanish treasure was layd up. Sr. Thomas Baskervile, Generall of the land-forces, undertook the service with seven hundred and fifty armed men. They marched through deep wayes, the Spaniards much annoying them with shot out of the woods. One fort in the passage they assaulted in vain, and heard that two others were built to stop them, besides Panama it self. They had so much of this breakfast, they thought they should surfet of a dinner and supper of the same. No hope of conquest, except with cloying the jaws of Death, and thrusting men on the mouth of the Canon. Wherefore fearing to find the Proverb true, That Gold may be bought too dear, they returned to their ships. Drake afterwards fired Nombre de Dios, and many other petty Towns (whose treasure the Spaniards had conveyed away) burning the empty casks, when their precious liquour was runne out before, and then prepared for their returning home.

Great was the difference betwixt the Indian cities now from what they were when Drake first haunted these coasts : At first the Spaniards here were safe and secure, counting their treasure sufficient to defend it self, the remotenesse thereof being the greatest (almost onely) resistance, and the fetching of it more then the fighting for it. Whilest the King of Spain guarded the head and heart of his dominions in Europe, he left his long legs in America open to blows, till finding them to smart, being beaten black and blew by the English, he learned to arm them at last, fortifying the most important of them to make them impregnable.

Now began Sr. Francis his discontent to feed upon him. He conceived that expectation, a mercilesse usurer, computing each day since his departure exacted an interest and return of honour and profit proportionable to his great pre- 10 parations, and transcending his former atchievements. He saw that all the good which he had done in this voyage, consisted in the evill he had done to the Spaniards afarre off, whereof he could present but small visible fruits in England. These apprehensions accompanying if not causing the disease of the flux wrought his sudden death. And sicknesse did not so much untie his clothes, as sorrow did rend at once the robe of his mortality asunder. He lived by the sea, died on it, and was buried in it. Thus an ex-tempore performance (scarce heard to be begun before we hear it is ended) comes 20 off with better applause, or miscarries with lesse disgrace, then a long studied and openly premeditated action. Besides, we see how great spirits, having mounted to the highest pitch of performance, afterwards strain and break their credits in striving to go beyond it. Lastly, God oftentimes leaves the brightest men in an eclipse, to shew that they do but borrow their lustre from his reflection. We will not justifie all the actions of any man, though of a tamer profession then a Sea-Captain, in whom civility is often counted precisenesse. For the main, we say that this our Captain 30 was a religious man towards God and his houses (generally sparing Churches where he came) chast in his life, just in his dealings, true of his word, and mercifull to those that were under him, hating nothing so much as idlenesse : And therefore lest his soul should rust in peace, at spare houres he brought fresh water to Plimouth. Carefull he was for posterity (though men of his profession have as well an ebbe of riot, as a flote of fortune) and providently raised a worshipfull Family of his kinred. In a word, should those that speak against him fast till they fetch their bread where he did his, they would have a good stomach to eat it.

(Book II, Chap. 21)

The true Gentleman

WE will consider him in his Birth, Breeding, and Behaviour.

10 *He is extracted from ancient and worshipfull parentage.* When a Pepin is planted on a Pepin-stock, the fruit growing thence is called a Renate, a most delicious apple, as both by Sire and Damme well descended. Thus his bloud must needs be well purified who is gentilely born on both sides.

If his birth be not, at leastwise his qualities are generous. What if he cannot with the Hevenninghams of Suffolk count five and twenty Knights of his familie, or tell sixteen Knights successively with the Tilneys of Norfolk, or with the Nauntons shew where their Ancestours had seven 20 hundred pound a yeare before or at the conquest ; yet he hath endeavoured by his own deserts to ennoble himself. Thus Valour makes him sonne to Cæsar, Learning entitles him kinsman to Tully, and Piety reports him nephew to godly Constantine. It graceth a Gentleman of low descent and high desert, when he will own the meannesse of his parentage. How ridiculous is it when many men brag, that their families are more ancient then the Moon, which all know are later then the starre which some seventy years since shined in Cassiopea. But if he be generously born, see how 30 his parents breed him.

He is not in his youth possest with the great hopes of his possession. No flatterer reads constantly in his ears a survey of the lands he is to inherit. This hath made many boyes thoughts swell so great they could never be kept in compasse afterwards. Onely his Parents acquaint him that he is the next undoubted Heir to correction, if misbehaving himself; and he finds no more favour from his Schoolmaster then his Schoolmaster finds diligence in him, whose rod respects persons no more then bullets are partiall in a battel. 10

At the University he is so studious as if he intended Learning for his profession. He knowes well that cunning is no burthen to carry, as paying neither portage by land, nor poundage by sea. Yea though to have land be a good First, yet to have learning is the surest Second, which may stand to it when the other may chance to be taken away.

At the Innes of Court he applyes himself to learn the Laws of the kingdome. Object not, Why should a Gentleman learn law, who if he needeth it may have it for his money, and if he 20 hath never so much of his own, he must but give it away. For what a shame is it for a man of quality to be ignorant of Solon in our Athens, of Lycurgus in our Sparta ? Besides, law will help him to keep his own, and besteed his neighbours. Say not, that there be enough which make this their set practice : for so there are also many masters of defence by their profession ; and shall private men therefore learn no skill at their weapons.

As for the Hospitality, the Apparell, the Travelling, the Companie, the Recreations, the Marriage of Gentlemen, they 30 are described in severall Chapters in the following Book. A word or two of his behaviour in the countrey.

He is courteous and affable to his neighbours. As the sword of the best tempered mettall is most flexible ; so the truly generous are most pliant and courteous in their behaviour to their inferiours.

He delights to see himself, and his servants well mounted : therefore he loveth good Horsemanship. Let never any forrein Rabshakeh send that brave to our Jerusalem, offering *to lend her two thousand horses, if she be able for her part to set riders upon them.* We know how Darius got the Persian Empire from the rest of his fellow Peeres, by the first neighing of his generous steed. It were no harm if in some needlesse suits of intricate precedencie betwixt equall Gentlemen, the priority were adjudged to him who keeps a stable of most serviceable horses.

He furnisheth and prepareth himself in peace against time of warre. Lest it be too late to learn when his skill is to be used. He approves himself couragious when brought to the triall, as well remembring the custome which is used at the Creation of Knights of the Bath, wherein the Kings Master-Cook cometh forth, and presenteth his great knife to the new-made Knights, admonishing them to be faithfull and valiant, otherwise he threatens them that that very knife is prepared to cut off their spurres.

If the Commission of the Peace finds him out, he faithfully discharges it. I say, Finds him out ; for a publick Office is a guest which receives the best usage from them who never invited it. And though he declined the Place, the countrey knew to prize his worth, who would be ignorant of his own. He compounds many petty differences betwixt his neighbours, which are easier ended in his own Porch then in Westminster-hall : for many people think, if once they have fetched a warrant from a Justice, they have given earnest to follow the suit, though otherwise the matter be so mean that the next nights sleep would have bound both parties to the peace, and made them as good friends as ever before. Yet

He connives not at the smothering of punishable faults. He hates that practice, as common as dangerous amongst countrey people, who having received again the goods which were stollen from them, partly out of foolish pity, and partly out of covetousnesse to save charges in prosecuting the law, let the thief escape unpunished. Thus whilest private losses are repaired, the wounds to the Commonwealth (in the breach of the Laws) are left uncured: And thus petty Larceners are encouraged into Felons, and afterwards are hang'd for pounds, because never whipt for pence, who, if they had felt the cord, had never been brought to the halter.

If chosen a Member of Parliament he is willing to do his Countrey service. If he be no Rhetorician to raise affections, (yea Barnabas was a greater speaker then S. Paul himself) he counts it great wisdome to be the good manager of Yea and Nay. The slow pace of his judgement is recompenced by the swift following of his affections, when his judgement is once soundly inform'd. And here we leave him in consultation, wishing him with the rest of his honourable Society all happy successe.

(Book II, Chap. 24)

Of Anger

ANGER is one of the sinews of the soul; he that wants it hath a maimed mind, and with Jacob sinew-shrunk in the hollow of his thigh must needs halt. Nor is it good to converse with such as cannot be angry, and with the Caspian sea never ebbe nor flow. This Anger is either Heavenly, when one is offended for God: or Hellish, when offended with God and Goodnes: or Earthly, in temporall matters. Which Earthly Anger (whereof we treat) may also be Hellish, if for no cause, no great cause, too hot, or too long.

Be not angry with any without a cause. If thou beest, thou must not onely, as the Proverb saith, be appeas'd without amends (having neither cost nor damage given thee) but, as our Saviour saith, be in danger of the judgement.

Be not mortally angry with any for a veniall fault. He will make a strange combustion in the state of his soul, who at the landing of every cockboat sets the beacons on fire. To be angry for every toy debases the worth of thy anger ; for he who will be angry for anything, will be angry for nothing.

Let not thy anger be so hot, but that the most torrid zone thereof may be habitable. Fright not people from thy pre-
10 sence with the terrour of thy intolerable impatience. Some men like a tiled house are long before they take fire, but once on flame there is no coming near to quench them.

Take heed of doing irrevocable acts in thy passion. As the revealing of secrets, which makes thee a bankrupt for society ever after : neither do such things which done once are done for ever, so that no bemoaning can amend them. Sampsons hair grew again, but not his eyes : Time may restore some losses, others are never to be repaird. Where-fore in thy rage make no Persian decree which cannot be
20 revers'd or repeald ; but rather Polonian laws which (they say) last but three dayes : Do not in an instant what an age cannot recompence.

Anger kept till the next morning, with Manna, doth putrifie and corrupt. Save that Manna corrupted not at all, and anger most of all, kept the next Sabbath. S. Paul saith, *Let not the Sunne go down on your wrath* ; to carry news to the Antipodes in another world of thy revengefull nature. Yet let us take the Apostles meaning, rather then his words, with all possible speed to depose our passion, not under-
30 standing him so literally that we may take leave to be angry till Sunset : then might our wrath lengthen with the dayes ; and men in Greenland, where day lasts above a quarter of a yeare, have plentifull scope of revenge. And as the English (by command from William the Conqueror) always

raked up their fire, and put out their candles, when the Curfew-bell was rung ; let us then also quench all sparks of anger and heat of passion.

He that keeps anger long in his bosome giveth place to the devil. And why should we make room for him, who will crowd in too fast of himself ? Heat of passion makes our souls to chappe, and the devil creeps in at the cranies ; yea a furious man in his fits may seem possess'd with a devil, fomes, fumes, tears himself, is deaf, and dumbe in effect, to heare or speak reason : sometimes wallows, stares, stamps, with fiery eyes and flaming cheeks. Had Narcissus himself seen his own face when he had been angry, he could never have fallen in love with himself.

(Book III, Chap. 8)

Of Books

Solomon saith truly, *Of making many Books there is no end*, so insatiable is the thirst of men therein : as also endles is the desire of many in buying and reading them. But we come to our Rules.

It is a vanity to perswade the world one hath much learning by getting a great library. As soon shall I believe every one is valiant that hath a well furnish'd armoury. I guesse good housekeeping by the smoking, not the number of the tunnels, as knowing that many of them (built merely for uniformity) are without chimnies, and more without fires. Once a dunce, void of learning but full of Books, flouted a library-lesse Scholar with these words, *Salve Doctor sine libris* : But the next day the Scholar coming into this jeerers study crowded with Books, *Salvete libri* (saith he) *sine Doctore.*

Few Books well selected are best. Yet as a certain Fool bought all the pictures that came out, because he might have his choice ; such is the vain humour of many men in gathering of Books : yet when they have done all, they misse their end, it being in the Editions of Authours as in the fashions of clothes, when a man thinks he hath gotten the latest and newest, presently another newer comes out.

Some Books are onely cursorily to be tasted of. Namely first Voluminous Books, the task of a mans life to reade them over ; secondly, Auxiliary Books, onely to be repair'd to on occasions ; thirdly, such as are mere pieces of Formality, so that if you look on them you look thorow them ; 10 and he that peeps thorow the casement of the Index sees as much as if he were in the house. But the lazinesse of those cannot be excused who perfunctorily passe over Authours of consequence, and onely trade in their Fables and Contents. These like City-Cheaters having gotten the names of all countrey Gentlemen, make silly people believe they have long lived in those places where they never were, and flourish with skill in those Authours they never seriously studied.

The Genius of the Authour is commonly discovered in the 20 *Dedicatory epistle.* Many place the purest grain in the mouth of the sack for chapmen to handle or buy : And from the dedication one may probably guesse at the Work, saving some rare and peculiar exceptions. Thus when once a Gentleman admired how so pithy, learned, and witty a dedication was match'd to a flat, dull, foolish book ; *In truth*, said another, *they may be well match'd together, for I professe they are nothing a kinne.*

Proportion an houres meditation to an houres reading of a staple Authour. This makes a man master of his learning, 30 and dispirits the book into the Scholar. The King of Sweden never filed his men above six deep in one company, because he would not have them lie in useless clusters in his Army, but so that every particular Souldier might be drawn out into service. Books that stand thinne on the shelves, yet so as the owner of them can bring forth every one of them into use, are better then farre greater libraries.

Learning hath gained most by those books by which the Printers have lost. Arius Montanus in printing the Hebrew Bible (commonly called the Bible of the King of Spain) much wasted himself, and was accused in the Court of Rome for his good deed, and being cited thither, *Pro tantorum laborum præmio vix veniam impetravit.* Likewise Christopher Plantin by printing of his curious interlineary Bible in Antwerp, through the unseasonable exactions of the Kings Officers, sunk and almost ruin'd his estate. And our worthy English Knight, who set forth the golden-mouth'd Father in a silver print, was a looser by it.

Whereas foolish Pamphlets prove most beneficiall to the Printers. When a French Printer complain'd that he was utterly undone by Printing a solid serious book of Rablais concerning Physick, Rablais to make him recompence made that his jesting scurrilous Work which repair'd the Printers losse with advantage. Such books the world swarms too much with. When one had set out a witlesse Pamphlet, writing *Finis* at the end thereof, another wittily wrote beneath it,

> ———*Nay there thou li'st, my friend,*
> *In writing foolish books there is no end.*

And surely such scurrilous scandalous papers do more then conceivable mischief. First their lusciousnesse puts many palats out of taste, that they can never after rellish any solid and wholsome Writers : secondly, they cast dirt on the faces of many innocent persons, which dryed on by continuance of time can never after be washed off : thirdly, the Pamphlets of this age may passe for Records with the next (because publickly uncontrolled) and what we laugh at, our children may believe : fourthly, grant the things true they jeer at, yet this musick is unlawfull in any

Christian Church, to play upon the sinnes and miseries of others, the fitter object of the Elegies then the Satyrs of all truly religious.

But what do I speaking against multiplicity of books in this age, who trespasse in this nature my self ? What was a learned mans complement may serve for my confession and conclusion, *Multi mei similes hoc morbo laborant, ut cum scribere nesciant tamen à scribendo temperare non possint.*

(Book III, Chap. 18)

Of Time-serving

THERE be foure kinds of Time-serving : first, out of Christian discretion, which is commendable ; second, out of humane infirmity, which is more pardonable ; third, and fourth, out of ignorance, or affectation, both which are damnable : of them in order.

He is a good Time-server that complyes his manners to the severall ages of this life : pleasant in youth, without wantonnesse ; grave in old age without frowardnesse. Frost is as proper for winter, as flowers for spring. Gravity becomes the ancient ; and a green Christmas is neither handsome nor healthfull.

He is a good Time-server that finds out the fittest opportunity for every action. God hath made a *time for every thing under the sunne,* save onely for that, which we do at all times, to wit Sinne.

He is a good Time-server that improves the present for Gods glory, and his own salvation. Of all the extent of time, onely the instant is that which we can call ours.

He is a good Time-server that is pliant to the times in matters of mere indifferency. Too blame are they whose minds may seem to be made of one entire bone without any joynts : they cannot bend at all, but stand as stiffly in things of pure indifferency, as in matters of absolute necessity.

He is a good Time-server that in time of persecution neither betrayes Gods cause, nor his own safety. And this he may do,

1 By lying hid both in his person and practice : though he will do no evil he will forbear the publick doing of some good. He hath as good cheer in his heart, though he keeps not open house, and will not publickly broch his Religion, till the palat of the times be better in taste to rellish it. *The Prudent shall keep silence in that time, for it is an evil time.* Though according to S. Peters command we are to *give a reason of our hope to every one that asketh* ; namely, that asketh for his instruction, but not for our destruction, especially if wanting lawfull Authority to examine us. *Ye shall be brought* saith Christ (no need have they therefore to run) *before Princes for my sake.*

2 By flying away : if there be no absolute necessity of his staying, no scandall given by his flight ; if he wants strength to stay it out till death ; and lastly, if God openeth a fair way for his departure : otherwise, if God bolts the doores and windows against him, he is not to creep out at the top of the chimney, and to make his escape by unwarrantable courses. If all should flie, Truth would want champions for the present ; if none should flie, Truth might want champions for the future. We come now to Time-servers out of infirmity.

Heart of oke hath sometimes warp'd a little in the scorching heat of persecution. Their want of true courage herein cannot be excused. Yet many censure them for surrendring up their forts after a long siege, who would have yielded up their own at the first summons. Oh, there is more required to make one valiant, then to call Cranmer or

Jewell Coward, as if the fire in Smithfield had been no hotter, then what is painted in the Book of Martyrs.

Yet afterwards they have come into their former straightnesse and stiffnesse. The troops which at first rather wheeld about then ran away have come in seasonable at last. Yea their constant blushing for shame of their former cowardlinesse hath made their souls ever after look more modest and beautifull. Thus Cranmer (who subscribed to Popery) grew valiant afterwards, and thrust his right hand which 10 subscribed first into fire, so that that hand dyed (as it were) a malefactour and all the rest of his body dyed a martyr.

Some have served the times out of mere Ignorance. Gaping for company, as others gap'd before them, *Pater noster,* or, Our Father. I could both sigh and smile at the witty simplicity of a poore old woman who had lived in the dayes of Queen Marie, and Queen Elizabeth, and said her prayers dayly both in Latine and English, and *Let God,* said she, *take to himself which he likes best.*

20   *But worst are those who serve the times out of mere Affectation.* Doing as the times do, not because the times do as they should do, but merely for sinister respects, to ingratiate themselves. We reade of an Earl of Oxford fined by King Henrie the seventh fifteen thousand marks for having too many Retainers. But how many Retainers hath Time had in all ages? and Servants in all offices? yea and Chaplains too?

It is a very difficult thing to serve the times; they change so frequently, so suddenly, and sometimes so violently 30 from one extreme to another. The times under Dioclesian were Pagan; under Constantine, Christian; under Constantius, Arian; under Julian, Apostate; under Jovian, Christian again, and all within the age of man, the term of seventie years. And would it not have wrench'd and

spraind his soul with short turning, who in all these should
have been of the Religion *for the time being* ?

Time-servers are oftentimes left in the lurch. If they do
not onely give their word for the times in their constant
discourses, but also give their bands for them, and write
in their defence. Such, when the times turn afterwards to
another extreme, are left in the briers, and come off very
hardly from the bill of their hands ; If they turn again
with the times none will trust them ; for who will make
a staff of an osier ? 10

*Miserable will be the condition of such Time-servers when
their Master is taken from them.* When as the Angel swore
Rev. 10. 6. that *Time shall be no longer.* Therefore is it
best serving of him who is eternity, a Master that can ever
protect us.

To conclude, he that intends to meet with one in a great
Fair, and knows not where he is, may sooner find him by
standing still in some principall place there, then by
traversing it up and down. Take thy stand on some good
ground in Religion, and keep thy station in a fixed posture, 20
never hunting after the times to follow them, and an
hundred to one, they will come to thee once in thy lifetime.

(Book III, Chap. 19)

The Life of Queen Elizabeth

WE intermeddle not with her description as she was a
Sovereigne Prince, too high for our pen, and performed by
others already, though not by any done so fully, but that
still room is left for the endeavours of Posterity to adde
thereunto. We consider her onely as she was a worthy
Lady, her private virtues rendring her to the imitation, and
her publick to the admiration of all.

Her royall birth by her Fathers side doth comparatively 30

make her Mother-descent seem low, which otherwise considered in it self was very noble and honourable. As for the bundle of scandalous aspersions by some cast on her birth, they are best to be buried without once opening of them. For as the basest rascall will presume to miscall the best Lord, when farre enough out of his hearing ; so slanderous tongues think they may run riot in railing on any, when once got out of the distance of time, and reach of confutation.

But Majesty which dyeth not will not suffer it self to be
10 so abused, seeing the best assurance which living Princes have, that their memories shall be honourably continued, is founded (next to their own deserts) in the maintaining of the unstained reputation of their Predecessours. Yea divine Justice seems herein to be a compurgatour of the parents of Queen Elizabeth, in that Nicholas Sanders, a Popish Priest, the first raiser of these wicked reports, was accidentally famished as he roved up and down in Ireland ; either because it was just he should be sterved that formerly surfeted with lying, or because that Iland out of a naturall
20 antipathy against poysonous creatures would not lend life to so venemous a slanderer.

Under the reigne of her Father, and Brother King Edward the sixth, (who commonly called her his Sister Temperance) she lived in a Princely fashion. But the case was altered with her when her Sister Mary came to the Crown, who ever look'd upon her with a jealous eye and frowning face : chiefly, because of the difference betwixt them in religion. For though Queen Mary is said of her self not so much as to have bark'd, yet she had under her
30 those who did more then bite ; and rather her religion then disposition was guilty in countenancing their cruelty by her authority.

This antipathy against her Sister Elizabeth was encreased with the remembrance how Katharine Dowager, Queen

Maries Mother, was justled out of the bed of Henry the
eighth by Anna Bullen, Mother to Queen Elizabeth : so
that these two Sisters were born, as I may say, not onely
in severall but opposite horizons, so that the elevation and
bright appearing of the one inferr'd the necessary obscurity
and depression of the other ; and still Queen Mary was
troubled with this *fit of the Mother*, which incensed her
against this her half Sister.

To which two grand causes of opposition, this third may
also be added, because not so generally known, though in
it self of lesser consequence. Queen Mary had released
Edward Courtney Earl of Devonshire out of the Tower,
where long he had been detained prisoner, a Gentleman of
a beautifull body, sweet nature, and royall descent, intending him, as it was generally conceived, to be an husband
for her self. For when the said Earl petitioned the Queen
for leave to travel she advised him rather to marry, ensuring
him that no Lady in the land, how high soever, would
refuse him for an husband ; and urging him to make his
choyce where he pleased, she pointed her self out unto him
as plainly as might stand with the modesty of a maid, and
Majesty of a Queen. Hereupon the young Earl (whether
because that his long durance had some influence on his
brain, or that naturally his face was better then his head,
or out of some private phancie and affection to the Lady
Elizabeth, or out of loyall bashfulnesse, not presuming to
climbe higher, but expecting to be call'd up) is said to have
requested the Queen for leave to marry her Sister the Lady
Elizabeth, unhappy that his choyce either went so high or
no higher : For who could have spoken worse Treason
against Mary (though not against the Queen) then to
preferre her Sister before her ? and she, innocent Lady, did
afterwards dearly pay the score of this Earls indiscretion.

For these reasons Lady Elizabeth was closely kept and

narrowly sifted all her Sisters reigne, Sr. Bedenifield her
keeper using more severity towards her then his place
required, yea more then a good man should, or a wiseman
would have done. No doubt the least tripping of her foot
should have cost her the losing of her head, if they could
have caught her to be privy to any conspiracies.

This Lady as well deserved the title of Elizabeth *the
Confessour* as ever Edward her ancient predecessour did.
Mr. Ascham was a good Schoolmaster to her, but affliction
10 was a better, so that it is hard to say whether she was more
happy in having a Crown so soon, or in having it no sooner,
till affliction had first laid in her a low (and therefore sure)
foundation of humility, for highnesse to be afterwards built
thereupon.

We bring her now from the Crosse to the Crown ; and
come we now to describe the rare endowments of her mind,
when behold her virtues almost stifle my pen, they crowd
in so fast upon it.

She was an excellent Scholar, understanding the Greek,
20 and perfectly speaking the Latine : witnesse her extempore
speech in answer to the Polish Embassadour, and another
at Cambridge, *Et si fœminilis iste meus pudor* (for so it
began) elegantly making the word *Fœminilis* : and well
might she mint one new word, who did refine so much new
gold and silver. Good skill she had in the French, and
Italian, using Interpreters not for need but state. She
was a good Poet in English, and fluently made verses.
In her time of persecution, when a Popish Priest pressed
her very hardly to declare her opinion concerning the pre-
30 sence of Christ in the Sacrament, she truly and warily
presented her judgement in these verses,

> *'Twas God the word that spake it,*
> *He took the bread and brake it ;*
> *And what the word did make it,*
> *That I believe and take it.*

And though perchance some may say this was but the best of shifts, and the worst of answers, because the distinct manner of the Presence must be believed ; yet none can deny it to have been a wise return to an adversary who lay at wait for all advantages. Nor was her Poetick vein lesse happy in Latine. When a little before the Spanish Invasion in eighty eight, the Spanish Embassadour (after a larger representation of his Masters demands) had summed up the effect thereof in a Tetrastich, she instantly in one verse rejoined her answer. We will presume to English both, though confessing the Latine loseth lustre by the Translation.

> *Te veto ne pergas bello defendere Belgas :*
> *Quæ Dracus eripuit nunc restituentur oportet :*
> *Quas Pater evertit jubeo te condere cellas :*
> *Relligio Papæ fac restituetur ad unguem.*

> These to you are our commands,
> Send no help to th' Netherlands :
> Of the treasure took by Drake,
> Restitution you must make :
> And those Abbies build anew,
> Which your Father overthrew :
> If for any peace you hope,
> In all points restore the Pope.

> The Queens extempore return,

> *Ad Græcas, bone Rex, fient mandata calendas.*

> Worthy King, know this your will
> At latter lammas wee'l fulfill.

Her piety to God was exemplary, none more constant or devout in private prayers ; very attentive also at Sermons, wherein she was better affected with soundnesse of matter, then queintnesse of expression : She could not well digest the affected over-elegancy of such as prayed for her by the title of *defendresse of the faith* and not the *Defender*, it being no false construction to apply a masculine word to so heroick a spirit.

She was very devout in returning thanks to God for her

constant and continuall preservations; for one traitours stabbe was scarce put by, before another took aim at her: But as if the poysons of treason by custome were turn'd naturall unto her, by Gods protection they did her no harm. In any designe of consequence she loved to be long, and well advised; but where her resolutions once seis'd, she would never let go her hold, according to her motto, *Semper eadem.*

By her Temperance she improved that stock of health which Nature bestowed on her, using little wine, and lesse Physick. Her Continence from pleasures was admirable, and she the Paragon of spotlesse chastity, what ever some Popish Priests (who count all virginity hid under a Nunnes veil) have feigned to the contrary. The best is, their words are no slander, whose words are all slander, so given to railing, that they must be dumbe if they do not blaspheme Magistrates. One Jesuit made this false Anagram on her name,

Elizabeth.
Jezabel.

false both in matter and manner. For allow it the abatement of H, (as all Anagrams must sue in Chancery for moderate favour) yet was it both unequall and ominous that T, a solid letter, should be omitted, the presage of the gallows whereon this Anagrammatist was afterwards justly executed.

Yea let the testimony of Pope Sixtus Quintus himself be believed, who professed that amongst all the Princes in Christendome he found but two which were worthy to bear command, had they not been stained with heresie, namely Henry the fourth, King of France, and Elizabeth Queen of England. And we may presume that the Pope, if commending his enemy, is therein infallible.

We come to her death, the discourse whereof was more welcome to her from the mouth of her private Confessour, then from a publick Preacher ; and she loved rather to tell her self, then to be told of her mortality, because the open mention thereof made (as she conceived) her subjects divide their loyalty betwixt the present and the future Prince. We need look into no other cause of her sicknesse then old age, being seventy years old (Davids age) to which no King of England since the Conquest did attain. Her weaknesse was encreased by her removall from London to Richmond in a cold winter day, sharp enough to pierce thorow those who were arm'd with health and youth. Also melancholy (the worst naturall Parasite, whosoever feeds him shall never be rid of his company) much afflicted her, being given over to sadnesse and silence.

Then prepared she her self for another world, being more constant in prayer, and pious exercises then ever before : yet spake she very little to any, sighing out more then she said, and making still musick to God in her heart. And as the red rose, though outwardly not so fragrant, is inwardly farre more cordiall then the damask, being more thrifty of its sweetnesse, and reserving it in it self ; so the religion of this dying Queen was most turn'd inward in soliloquies betwixt God and her own soul, though she wanted not outward expressions thereof. When her speech fail'd her, she spake with her heart, tears, eyes, hands, and other signes, so commending herself to God the best interpreter, who understands what his Saints desire to say. Thus dyed Queen Elizabeth, whilest living, the first maid on earth, and when dead, the second in heaven.

Surely the kingdome had dyed with their Queen, had not the fainting spirits thereof been refresh'd by the coming in of gratious King James.

She was of person, tall ; of hair and complexion, fair,

well-favoured, but high-nosed ; of limbes and feature, neat ;
of a stately and majestick deportment. She had a piercing
eye wherewith she used to touch what metall strangers were
made of, which came into her presence. But as she counted
it a pleasant conquest with her Majestick look to dash
strangers out of countenance, so she was mercifull in pursuing those whom she overcame, and afterwards would
cherish and comfort them with her smiles, if perceiving
towardlinesse, and an ingenuous modesty in them. She
10 much affected rich and costly apparell ; and if ever jewells
had just cause to be proud, it was with her wearing them.

(Book IV, Chap. 15)

THE PROFANE STATE

The Hypocrite

By *Hypocrite* we understand such a one as doth (Isaiah
32. 6.) *practise hypocrisie*, make a trade or work of dissembling : For otherwise, *Hypocriseorum macula carere,
aut paucorum est aut nullorum*. The best of Gods children
have a smack of hypocrisie.

*An Hypocrite is himself both the archer and the mark, in
all actions shooting at his own praise or profit*. And therefore
he doth all things that they may be seen : What with
20 others is held a principall point in Law, is his main Maxime
in Divinity, To have good witnesse. Even fasting it self
is meat and drink to him, whilest others behold it.

In the outside of religion he out-shines a sincere Christian.
Guilt cups glitter more then those of massie gold, which
are seldome burnish'd. Yea, well may the Hypocrite afford
gaudy facing, who cares not for any lining ; brave it in the
shop, that hath nothing in the ware-house. Nor is it a
wonder if in outward service he out-strips Gods servants,

who out-doeth Gods command by will-worship, giving God more then he requires, though not what most he requires, I mean, his heart.

His vizard is commonly pluckt off in this world. Sincerity is an entire thing in it self : Hypocrisie consists of severall pieces cunningly closed together ; and sometimes the Hypocrite is smote (as Ahab with an arrow, 1 Kings 22. 34.) betwixt the joynts of his armour, and so is mortally wounded in his reputation. Now by these shrewd signes a dissembler is often discovered : First : heavie censuring of others for light faults : secondly, boasting of his own goodnesse : thirdly, the unequall beating of his pulse in matters of pietie, hard, strong and quick, in publick actions ; weak, soft and dull, in private matters : fourthly, shrinking in persecution ; for painted faces cannot abide to come nigh the fire.

Yet sometimes he goes to the grave neither detected nor suspected. If Masters in their art, and living in peaceable times wherein pietie and prosperity do not fall out, but agree well together. Maud, mother to King Henry the second, being besieged in Winchester castle, counterfeited herself to be dead, and so was carried out in a coffin whereby she escaped. Another time being besieged at Oxford in a cold winter, with wearing white apparell she got away in the snow undiscovered. Thus some Hypocrites by dissembling mortification that they are dead to the world, and by professing a snow-like purity in their conversations, escape all their life time undiscerned by mortall eyes.

By long dissembling piety he deceives himself at last : Yea, he may grow so infatuated as to conceive himself no dissembler but a sincere Saint. A scholar was so possessed with his lively personating of King Richard the third, in a Colledge-Comedy, that ever after he was transported with a royall humour in his large expences, which brought him to beggery, though he had great preferment. Thus the Hypocrite by long acting the part of piety, at last believes himself really to be such an one, whom at first he did but counterfeit.

God here knows, and hereafter will make Hypocrites known to the whole world. Ottocar King of Bohemia refused to do homage to Rodulphus the first, Emperour, till at last, chastised with warre, he was content to do him homage privately in a tent ; which tent was so contrived by the 10 Emperours servants, that by drawing one cord, it was all taken away, and so Ottocar presented on his knees doing his homage, to the view of three Armies in presence. Thus God at last shall uncase the closest dissembler to the fight of men angels and devils, having removed all veils and pretences of piety : no goat in a sheepskin shall steal on his right hand at the last day of judgement.

(Book V, Chap. 8)

The Degenerous Gentleman

SOME will chalenge this title of incongruity, as if those two words were so dissonant, that a whole sentence cannot hold them ; for sure where the Gentleman is the root, 20 Degenerous cannot be the fruit. But if any quarrell with my words, Valerius Maximus shall be my champion, who styleth such, *Nobilia Portenta*. By *Gentleman* we understand one whom the Heralds (except they will deny their best Records) must allow of ancient parentage. Such a one, when a child, being kept the devils Nazarite, that no razor of correction must come upon his head in his fathers family, see what he proves in the processe of time, brought to extreme poverty. Herein we intend no invective glance on those pious Gentlemen, whose states are consumed 30 through Gods secret judgement, and none of the owners

visible default ; onely we meddle with such as by careles-
nesse and riot cause their own ruine.

He goes to school to learn in jest and play in earnest. Now
this Gentleman, now that Gentlewoman begges him a play-
day, and now the book must be thrown away, that he may
see the buck hunted. He comes to school late, departs
soon, and the whole yeare with him (like the fortnight
when Christmas day falls on a tuesday) is all Holidayes
and half-Holidayes. And as the Poets feigne of Thetis, that
she drench'd Achilles her sonne in the Stygian waters, that
he might not be wounded with any weapon ; so cockering
mothers inchant their sonnes to make them rod-free, which
they do by making some golden circles in the hand of the
Schoolmaster : thus these two conjoyning together make
the indentures to bind the youth to eternall ignorance ;
yet perchance he may get some almes of learning, here
a snap, there a piece of knowledge, but nothing to purpose.

His fathers Servingmen (which he counts no mean prefer-
ment) admit him into their society. Going to a drinking
match they carry him with them to enter him, and applaud
his hopefulnesse, finding him vicious beyond his age. The
Butler makes him free (having first pai'd his fees accustomed) of his own fathers cellar, and guesseth the profound-
nesse of his young masters capacity by the depth of the
whole-ones he fetcheth off.

Coming to the University, his chief study is to study nothing.
What is Learning but a cloakbag of books, cumbersome for
a Gentleman to carry ? and the Muses fit to make wives
for Farmers sonnes : perchance his own Tutour, for the
promise of the next living (which notwithstanding his
promise he afterwards sells to another) contributes to his
undoing, letting him live as he list : yea, perhaps his own
mother (whilest his father diets him for his health with
a moderate allowance) makes him surfet underhand by

sending him money. Thus whilest some complain that the
University infected him, he infected the Universitie, from
which he suck'd no milk but poysoned her nipples.

*At the Innes of Court under pretence to learn Law, he learns
to be lawlesse* ; not knowing by his study so much as what
an Execution means, till he learns it by his own dear
experience. Here he grows acquainted with the *Roaring
Boyes*, I am afraid so called by a wofull Prolepsis, Here,
for Hereafter. What formerly was counted the chief credit
of an Oratour, these esteem the honour of a Swearer, *Pro-
nunciation*, to mouth an oath with a gracelesse grace.
These (as David saith) *cloath themselves with curses as with
a garment*, and therefore desire to be in the latest fashion
both in their cloaths and curses : These infuse all their
skill into their young novice, who shortly proves such a
proficient, that he exceeds his Masters in all kinds of
vicious courses.

*Through the mediation of a Scrivener he grows acquainted
with some great Usurer*. Nor is this youngster so ravenous,
as the other is ready to feed him with money, sometimes
with a courteous violence forcing on him more then he
desires, provided the security be good, except the Usurer
be so valiant as to hazard the losing of a small hook to
catch a great fish, and will adventure to trust him, if his
estate in hope be overmeasure, though he himself be under
age. Now the greater part of the money he takes up is not
for his own spending, but to pay the shot of other mens riot.

After his fathers death he flies out more then ever before.
Formerly he took care for means for his spending, now he
takes care for spending for his means. His wealth is so
deep a gulf, no riot can ever sound the bottome of it. To
make his guests drunk is the onely seal of their welcome.
His very meanest servant may be master of the cellar, and
those who deserve no beere may command the best wine :

such dancing by day, such masking by night, such roaring, such revelling, able to awake the sleeping ashes of his Great-great-grandfather, and to fright all blessing from his house.

Mean time the old soare of his London-debts corrupts and festers. He is carelesse to take out the dead flesh, or to discharge either principall or interest. Such small leaks are not worth the stopping or searching for till they be greater ; he should undervalue himself to pay a summe before it grew considerable for a man of his estate. Nor can he be more carelesse to pay, then the Usurer is willing to continue the debt, knowing that his bands, like infants, battle best with sleeping.

Vacation is his vocation, and he scorns to follow any profession ; and will not be confin'd to any laudable employment. But they who count a calling a prison, shall at last make a prison their calling. He instills also his lazie principles into his children, being of the same opinion with the Neapolitane Gentry, who stand so on the puntoes of their honour, that they preferre robbery before industry, and will rather suffer their daughter to make merchandise of her chastity, then marry the richest merchant.

Drinking is one of the principall Liberall Sciences he professeth. A most ungentile quality, fit to be banished to rogues and rags. It was anciently counted a Dutch vice, and swarmed most in that countrey. I remember a sad accident which hapned to Fliolmus King of Gothland, who whilest a Lord of misrule in his Court, and both he and his servants were drunk, in mere merriment, meaning no harm, they took the King and put him in jest into a great vessel of beere, and drowned him in earnest. But one tells us that this ancient and habited vice is amongst the Dutch of late years much decreased : which if it be not, would it were. Sure our Mariners observe that as the sea grows

dayly shallower and shallower on the shoars of Holland
and Zeland, so the channell of late waxeth deeper on the
coasts of Kent and Essex. I pray God if drunkennesse
ebbes in Dutchland, it doth not flow in England, and gain
not in the Iland what it loseth in the Continent. Yea some
plead, when overwhelm'd with liquour, that their thirst is
but quenched : as well may they say, that in Noahs floud
the dust was but sufficiently allayed.

Gaming is another art he studies much : an enticing witch,
10 that hath caused the ruine of many. Hanniball said of
Marcellus, that *nec bonam nec malam fortunam ferre potest,*
he could be quiet neither conquerour nor conquered ; thus
such is the itch of play, that Gamesters neither winning
nor losing can rest contented. One propounded this question, Whether men in ships on sea were to be accounted
among the living or the dead, because there were but few
inches betwixt them and drowning. The same scruple may
be made of great Gamesters, though their estates be never
so great, whether they are to be esteemed poore or rich,
20 there being but a few casts at dice betwixt a Gentleman
(in great game) and a begger. Our Gallant games deeply,
and makes no doubt in conscience to adventure Advousands,
Patronages, and Church-livings in gaming. He might call
to mind Sr. Miles Pateridge, who (as the Souldiers cast lots
for Christ his coat) plaid at dice for Jesus bells with King
Henry the eighth, and wonne them of him. Thus he
brought the bells to ring in his pocket, but the ropes afterwards catch'd about his neck, and for some offenses he was
hang'd in the dayes of King Edward the sixth.

30 *Then first he sells the outworks of his state, some stragling
mannour.* Nor is he sensible of this sale, which makes his
means more entire, as counting the gathering of such
scattering rents rather burdensome then profitable. This
he sells at half the value, so that the feathers will buy the

goose, and the wood will pay for the ground : with this money if he stops the hole to one Creditour, by his prodigality he presently opens a wider gappe to another.

By this time the long dormant Usurer ramps for the payment of his money. The Principall, the grandmother, and the Use, the daughter, and the Use upon use, the grandchild, and perchance a generation farther, hath swell'd the debt to an incredible summe, for the satisfying whereof our Gallant sells the moity of his estate.

Having sold half his land he abates nothing of his expenses : but thinks five hundred pounds a yeare will be enough to maintain that for which a thousand pound was too little. He will not stoop till he falls, nor lessen his kennell of dogs, till with Acteon he be eaten up with his own hounds.

Being about to sink he catcheth at every rush to save himself. Perchance sometimes he snatcheth at the thistle of a project, which first pricks his hands, and then breaks. Herein it may be he adventured on a matter wherein he had no skill himself (hoping by letting the Commonwealth bloud to fill up his own veins again) and therefore trades with his partners brains, as his partner with his purse, till both miscarry together : or else it may be he catcheth hold on the heel of another man, who is in as dangerous a case as himself, and they embracing each other in mutuall bands hasten their drowning together. His last mannour he sells twice, to a countrey-Gentleman, and a London-usurer, though the last, as having the first title, prevails to possesse it : Usurers herein being like unto Foxes ; they seldome take pains to digge any holes themselves, but earth in that which the foolish Badger made for them, and dwell in the mannours and fair houses which others have built and provided.

Having lost his own legs, he relyes on the staff of his kinred ; first visiting them as an intermitting ague, but afterwards

turns a quotidian, wearing their thresholds as bare as his
own coat. At last he is as welcome as a storm ; he that
is abroad shelters himself from it, and he that is at home
shuts the doore.   If he intrudes himself, yet some with
their jeering tongues give him many a gird, but his brazen
impudence feels nothing ; and let him be arm'd on free-
cost with the pot and the pipe, he will give them leave to
shoot their flouts at him till they be weary. Sometimes he
sadly paceth over the ground he sold, and is on fire with
10 anger with himself for his folly, but presently quencheth
it at the next ale-house.

Having undone himself, he sets up the trade to undoe others.
If he can but scrue himself into the acquaintance of a rich
heir, he rejoyceth as much at the prize as the Hollanders
when they had intercepted the Plate-Fleet.   He tutours
this young Gamester in vice, leading him a more com-
pendious way to his ruine then possibly he could find out
of himself.   And doth not the guide deserve good wages
for his direction ?

20   *Perhaps he behaves himself so basely that he is degraded* ;
the sad and solemn Ceremonies whereof we may meet with
in old Presidents : but of them all, in my apprehension,
none should make deeper impression in an ingenuous soul
then this one, That at the solemn degradation of a Knight
for high misdemeanour, the King and twelve Knights more
did put on mourning garments, as an embleme of sorrow
for this injury to honour, that a man Gentile by birth and
bloud, or honoured by a Princes favour, should so farre
forget not onely himself but his Order, as to deserve so
30 severe punishment.

His death is as miserable, as his life hath been vicious. An
Hospitall is the height he hopes to be advanced to : But
commonly he dies not in so charitable a prison, but sings
his last note in a cage.   Nor is it impossible, but that

wanting land of his own he may incroch on the Kings high-
way, and there, taking himself to be Lord of the soyl, seise
on Travellers as Strayes due unto him, and so the hangman
give him a wreath more then he had in his Armes before.
If he dyes at liberty in his pilgrimage betwixt the houses
of his acquaintance, perhaps some well-disposed Gentleman
may pay for his buriall, and truly mourn at the funerall of
an ancient Family. His children, if any, must seek their
fortunes the farther off, because their father found his too
soon, before he had wisdome to manage them. Within 10
two generations his name is quite forgotten that ever any
such was in the place, except some Herald in his visitation
passe by, and chance to spell his broken Arms in a Church-
window. And then how weak a thing is Gentry, then
which (if it wants virtue) brittle glasse is the more lasting
monument ?

We forbear to give an instance of a degenerous Gentleman ; would to God the world gave no examples of them.
If any please to look into the forenamed Valerius Maximus,
he shall there find the base son of Scipio Africanus, the 20
conquerour of Hanniball and Africk, so ill imitating his
father, that for his viciousnes he received many disgracefull
repulses from the people of Rome, the fragrant smell of his
Fathers memory making him to stink the more in their
nostrils ; yea they forced him to pluck off from his finger
a signet-ring, whereon the face of his Father was engraven,
as counting him unworthy to wear his picture who would
not resemble his virtue.

(Book V, Chap. 14)

GOOD THOUGHTS
IN
BAD TIMES,

Consisting of

Personall Meditations.
Scripture Observations.
Historicall Applications.
Mixt Contemplations.

By THOMAS FULLER.

PSAL. 4. 4.
*Commune with your hearts in
your Chamber, and be still.*

EXETER,
Printed for *Thomas Hunt,*
1645.

Lord,

I DO discover a Fallacy, whereby I have long deceived my self. Which is this : I have desired to begin my Amendment, from my Birth day, or from the first day of the Yeer, or from some Eminent Festivall, that so my Repentance might bear some Remarkable date. But when those dayes were come, I have adjourned my Amendment to some other Time. Thus whilst I could not agree with my self when to Start, I have almost lost the Running of the Race. I am resolved thus to befool my self no longer. I see no day to *To day*, the instant Time is alwayes the fittest time. In *Nabuchadnezars* Image, the lower the Members, the Courser the Mettall, the further off the Time, the more unfit. To day is the Golden Opportunity, to Morrow will be the Silver Season, next day, but the Brazen one, and so long, till at last I shall come to the *Toes* of *Clay*, and be turned to dust. Grant therefore that *to day I may hear thy voice*. And if this day be obscure in the Kallender, and remarkable in it self for nothing else, give me to make it memorable in my soul, thereupon, by thy Assistance, begining the Reformation of my life.

(*Personall Meditations*, viii.)

Lord,

WHEN I am to Travell, I never use to provide my self, till the very Tyme ; Partly out of Lazinesse, loath to be troubled till needs I must, partly out of Pride, as presuming all necessaries for my Journey will wait upon me at the instant. (Some say this is Schollers fashion, and it seemes by following it, I hope to approve my self to be one). However, it often comes to passe, that my Journey is finally stopt, through the Narrownesse of the Time to provide for it. Grant, Lord, that my confess'd Improvidence in Temporall, may make me suspect my Providence in Spirituall Matters. *Salomon* saith, *Man goeth to his long*

Home. Short Preparation will not fit so long a Journey.
O ! let me not put it off to the last, to have my Oile to buy,
when I am to burn it. But let me so dispose of my self, that
when I am to dye, I may have nothing to do but to dye.

(Personall Meditations, xvi)

Lord,

WHEN in any writing, I have occasion to insert these
passages, *God willing, God lending me life, &c.* I observe,
Lord, that I can scarce hold my hand from incircling these
words in a Parenthesis, as if they were not Essentiall to
10 the Sentence, but may as well be left out, as put in. Whereas indeed they are not onely of the *Commission at large,*
but so of the *Quorum*, that without them all the rest is
nothing, wherefore hereafter, I will write those words fully
and fairely without any Inclosure about them. Let Criticks
censure it for bad Grammer, I am sure it is good Divinity.

(Personall Meditations, xvii)

Lord,

THIS day I disputed with my self, whether or no I had
said my Prayers this Morning ; And I could not call to
mind any remarkable Passage, whence I could certainly
20 conclude that I had offered my Prayers unto thee. Frozen
Affections, which left no Spark of Remembrance behind
them. Yet at last I hardly recovered one Token, whence
I was assured that I had said my Prayers. It seems I had
said them, and *onely said them*, rather by heart then with
my heart. Can I hope that thou wouldest Remember my
Prayers, when I had almost forgotten that I had prayed ?
Or rather have I not Cause to fear, that thou remembrest
my Prayers too well, to punish the Coldnesse and Badnesse
of them ? Alas, are not Devotions thus done, in effect left
30 undone. Well *Iacob* advised his Sonnes, at their second
going into Egypt, Take double Money in your hand; per-
adventure it was an Oversight. So, Lord, I come with my

second Morning Sacrifice : Be pleased to accept it, which I desire, and endeavour to present, with a little better Devotion, then I did the former.

(Personall Meditations, xix)

Lord,

BE pleased to shake my Clay Cottage, before thou throwest it down. May it totter a while, before it doth Tumble. Let me be summon'd before I am surpriz'd. Deliver me from *Sudden Death*. Not from Sudden Death, in respect of it self, for I care not how short my passage be, so it be safe. Never any weary Traveller Complained, that he came too soon to his Journeys end. But let it not be Sudden in respect of me. Make me always ready to receive Death. Thus no Guest comes unawares to him, who keeps a Constant Table.

(Personall Meditations, xxv)

Lord,

I DISCOVER an arrant Lazinesse in my Soul. For when I am to read a Chapter in thy Bible before I begin it, I look where it endeth. And if it endeth not on the same side, I cannot keep my hands, from turning over the leaf, to measure the length thereof on the other side ; If it swels to many Verses I begin to grudge. Surely my heart is not rightly affected. Were I truly hungry after heavenly Food, I would not Complain of the greatest Messe of Meat. Scourge, Lord, this Lazinesse, out of my Soul, make the reading of thy Word, not a Penance, but a Pleasure unto me. Teach me, that as amongst many heaps of Gold, all being equally pure, that is the best, which is the biggest, so I may esteem that Chapter in thy Word, the best that is the Longest.

(Scripture Observations, xxi)

I PERCEIVE there is in the world a good Nature, falsely so called, as being nothing else, but a facill and flexible *Disposition*, wax for every impression. What others are so

bold to beg, they are so bashfull as not to deny. Such
Osiers, can never make Beams to bear Stresse, in Church
and State. If this be *good Nature*, let me alwayes be a
Clown. If this be *good Fellowship*, let me alwayes be a
Churle. Give me to set a Sturdy *Porter* before my Soul, who
may not equally open to every Commer. I cannot conceive,
how he can be a *Friend to any*, who is a friend to all, and
the worst *Foe to himself*.   (*Mixt Contemplations*, xiii)

HA, is the Interjection of Laughter. *Ah*, is an Interjection of Sorrow. The difference betwixt them very
small, as consisting onely in the Transposition of what is no
Substantiall Letter, but a bare Aspiration. How quickly in
the Age of a Minute, in the very turning of a Breath, is our
Mirth chang'd into Mourning.   (*Mixt Contemplations*, xiv)

WHEN a Child, I loved to look on the Pictures in the
Book of Martyrs. I thought that there the Martyres at the
Stake, seemed like the three Children in the fiery Fournace.
Ever since I had known them there, *not one hair more of
their Head was burnt, nor any smell of the fire singeing of
their Cloaths*. This made me think Martyrdom was nothing.
But O, though *the Lion be painted fiercer then he is*, the fire
is farre fiercer then it is painted. Thus it is easie for one
to endure an affliction, as hee limnes it out in his own
fancie, and represents it to himself but in a bare Specula-
tion. But when it is brought indeed, and laied home to
us, there must be the Man, yea, there must be more then
the Man, yea, there must be God to assist the Man to
undergo it.   (*Mixt Contemplations*, xxi)

TRAVELLING on the *Plain*, (which notwithstanding hath
its *Risings* and *Fallings*) I discovered *Salisbury* Steeple
many miles off : Coming to a declivity, I lost the sight

thereof : But climbing up the next Hill, the Steeple grew
out of the Ground again. Yea, I often found it, and lost it,
till at last, I came safely to it, and took my lodging neer it.
It fareth thus with us, whilst we are wayfairing to heaven,
mounted on the Pisgah Top of some good Meditation, we
get a glimps of our Celestiall *Canaan*. But when, either
on the Flat of an Ordinary Temper, or in the Fall of an
Extraordinary Temptation, we lose the view thereof.
Thus, in the sight of our Soul, Heaven is discovered,
covered and recovered, till, though late, at last, though 10
slowly, surely, we arrive at the Haven of our Happinesse.

(*Mixt Contemplations*, xxii)

Lord,

I FIND my self in the *Latitude* of a *Feaver*. I am neither
well, nor ill. Not so well, that I have any mind to be
merry with my Friends, nor so ill that my Friends have any
cause to Condole with me. I am a *Probationer* in point of
my health. As I shall behave my self, so I may be either
expelled out of it, or admitted into it. Lord, let my dis-
temper stop here, and go no further. Shoot not thy
Murthering Pieces against that Clay-Castle, which sur- 20
rendreth it self at thy first Summons. *O spare me a little !*
that I may recover my strength. I begge not to be forgiven,
but to be forborn my *Debt to Nature*. And I onely do *crave*
time, for a while, till I be better fitted, and furnished to pay it.

(*Mixt Contemplations*, xxiii)

GOOD THOUGHTS IN WORSE
TIMES 1647
Bare in fat Pasture

FORRESTERS have informed mee, that *Outlodging Deere*
are seldom seen to be so fat as those as keep themselves
within the Parke. Whereof they assigne this Reason that

those Straglers though they have more ground to range over, more Grass, and Grain, to take their repast upon, yet they are in constant feare as if conscious, that they are *Trespassers*, eing out of the *Protection*, because out of the *Pale* of the *Parke*. This makes their *Eyes* and *Eares* alwayes to stand *Sentinels* for their *mouthes*, lest the Master of the ground pursue them for the damage done unto him.

Are there any which unjustly possesse the Houses of others? Surely such can never with quiet and comfort enjoy either their places or themselves. They alwayes listen to the least Noise of Newes, suspecting the *Right owner* should be reestated, whose restitution of necessity inferres the others Ejection. Lord, grant that though my meanes be never so small, grant they may be *my meanes*, not wrongfully detained from others, having a truer Title unto them.

(*Meditations on the Times*, ix)

MIXT CONTEMPLATIONS IN BETTER TIMES 1660

An ill Match

DIVINE Providence is remarkable in ordering, that a *Fog* and a *Tempest* never did, nor can, meet together in nature. For as soon as a *Fogg* is *fixed*, the *Tempest* is *allaid*; and as soon as a *Tempest* doth arise, the *Fogg* is *dispersed*. This is a great mercy, for otherwise such small vessels as boats and barges, which want the conduct of the *Card* and *Compass*, would irrecoverably be lost.

How sad then is the condition of many Sectaries in our age; which in the same instant have a *Fogg* of *ignorance* in their *judgments*, and a *Tempest* of *violence* in their *affections*, being too *blind* to *go right*, and yet too *active* to *stand* still.

(V)

Sad Transposition

IT seemeth marvellous to me, that many *Mechanicks* (few able to read, and fewer to write their names) turning *Souldiers*, and *Captains* in our *Warrs*, should be so soon and so much improved. They seeme to me to have *commenced per saltum* in their understandings. I professe without flouting *or* flattering, I have much admired, with what facilitie and fluentnesse, how pertinently and properly they have expressed themselves, in language which they were never borne nor bred to, but have industriously acquired by conversing with their betters.   10

What a *shame* would it be, if such who have been of *Gentile Extraction*, and have had *liberal education*, should (as if it were by *exchange of Soules*) relapse into *Ignorance* and *Barbarism*.

What an *ignominy* would it be for them, to be buried in idleness, and in the immoderate pursuite of pleasures and vicious courses, till they besot their understandings, when they see Souldiers arrived at such an improvement, who were bred *Taylors*, *Shoe-makers*, *Coblers*, &c.

Not that I write this (God knoweth my heart) in disgrace 20 of them, because they were bred in so meane Callings, which are both honest in themselves, and usefull in the *Commonwealth* ; yea, I am so farr from thinking ill of them, for being bred in so *poor trades*, that I should think better of them for returning *unto them* againe.

(XVII)

Trusting maketh one Trusty

(From the mouth of my worthie Friend, now gon to God, D. Clare Chaplain then to his Highnesse.)

CHARLES the Second, *King* of the *Scots*, when a Childe was much troubled with a weaknesse in his Legs, and was appointed to weare STEEL-BOOTES, for the strengthening of them.

The weights of these so clogged the Childe, that he enjoyed not himself in any degree, but moaned himself, *fasting* at *feasts*, yea, his *very Play* being *work* unto him, he may be said to be a *Prisoner* in his own *Palace*.

It hapned that an *Aged Rocker* which waited on him, took the STEEL-BOOTS from his legs, and cast them in a place, where it was *hard* to *find* them *there*, and *impossible* to *fetch* them *thence*, promising the *Countess* of *Dorset*, (*Governess* of the *Prince*) that if any Anger arised thereof, she would take all the blame on her self.

Not long after, the King coming into the *Nursery*, and beholding the BOOTS taken from his legs, was offended thereat, demanding in some anger, Who had done it :

It was I Sir (said the *Rocker*) *who had the honour (some thirty years since) to attend on your Highness in your Infancie, when you had the same infirmity wherewith now the Prince, (your very own Son) is troubled. And then, the Lady* Cary, (afterward *Countess* of *Monmouth*) *commanded your* STEEL BOOTS *to be taken off, who, blessed be God, since have gathered strength, and arrived at a good stature.*

The Nation is too Noble, when his *MAIESTY*, (who hitherto hath had *a short course, but a long Pilgrimage,*) shall return from forreign parts, to impose any other STEEL BOOTS upon him, then the observing the *Lawes of the Land*, which are his *own stockings*, that so with joy and comfort he may enter on what was his own inheritance.

But I remember, when *Luther* began first to mistake some Errours in the *Romish Church*, and complained thereof to *Staupitius* his Confessor, He used to say unto him. *Abi in Cellam & ora, Get you gone into your Cell and pray.* So will I do, (who have now done) and leave the managing of the rest to those to whom it is most proper to advance Gods Glory, and their Countreys good. *Amen.*

(L)

A Pisgah-sight of

PALESTINE

and

The CONFINES thereof

1650.

Phœnicia

Phœnicia is often mentioned in Scripture, and is so called as some will have it ἀπὸ τῶν φοινίκων, from plenty of Palm-trees growing therein ; as others παρὰ τὸ φόνος, from the many slaughters formerly made in that warlike Nation. To omit other antiquated deductions thereof, prettiest (because newest) is that of a modern Author from בני ענק *bhene-Anak, Pheanak, Phœnik, the sons of Anak,* as the fathers and founders of the People of this Country. A long slender Country it is, having the bounds thereof by severall Authors variously assigned ; but generally extended from the Sea 10 to Mount *Libanus* in breadth, and in length from *Carmel* to the River *Canis* in the North ; a tract of an hundred miles and upwards.

The Inhabitants hereof were transcendently ingenious ; whose wits (like the Gold wire they so much dealt with) were ductile and pliable to all inventions. From a pin to a pillar, nothing was so small but their skill could work ; nothing so great but their industry could atchieve. What-soever was pretty for children to play with, or neat for women to wear, or necessary for man to use, in any one of 20 these the *Phœnicians* were so expert, Nature might seem

to design them for that alone, and so dextrous in all of
them, it were hard to say wherein they excelled. They
could weave clothes with the smallest thred, dress them
with the finest work, dye them with the freshest colours,
embroider them with the richest cost, and then either sell
them to others to their great profit, or wear them with as
much pride themselves. They were excellent Architects;
Solomon himself (who well knew the most cunning workmen
in every craft) confessing to *Hiram, There is not amongst us*
10 *any that have skill to hew Timber like the Sidonians.* They
are also conceived the first founders of Letters, Arithmetick,
Astronomy, with the working in glass, and severall other
rare devices.

   Tyre was the chiefest City in *Phœnicia, situate at the
entrance of the Sea.* Elegantly the Prophet termeth *the
Harvest of the River her revenue* : an Harvest lasting all
the year long, every day sowing at the setting forth, and
reaping at the return of her Ships. *Tyre* said to her self
I am of perfect beauty, which coming out of her own mouth
20 was rather proudly than falsly spoken. If it be accounted
one of the stateliest sights in the world, to see a stout Ship
under sale, how beautifull was it to behold the *Tyrian*
Gallies with all their accoutrements ; Planks of the Fir-
trees of *Senir,* Masts of the Cedars of *Lebanon,* Oars of the
Oaks of *Bashan,* Hatches of the Ivory of *Chittim,* Sails with
broidered work (oh vanity top and top gallant !) out of
Egypt, blue and purple Carpets for covering from the Iles
of *Elisha,* with *Giblites* for Calkers, *Arvadites* for Mariners,
Persians, &c. for Souldiers, and *Tyrians,* her own townsmen
30 for *Pilots,* so keeping the honour, and haply seeking to preserve the mysteries of their harbour to themselves ?

   Pass we from their Ships to their Shops, which we find
fraught with commodities of all kinds. Whose *Merchants
are Princes* saith the Prophet ; and it seems that *Tyrannus*

a good word for a good King (till customary using thereof
in the worst sense infected it) had its originall from the
Pride and Magnificence of the *Tyrian* Merchants. This City
is termed *a Mart of Nations*, both because all Nations were
there to sell, and there to be sold : *they traded the persons
of men*, and not only Arms but Armies were here to be
bought, and *Horsemen as well as Horses* were chaffered in
their Markets.

Now as *Tyre* was dispersed all over the world in the
severall Colonies planted by her in foraign parts ; so the
World was contracted into *Tyre*, whither Merchants from
all Countries did repair. Compare *Ezek*. 27. with *Gen*. 10
and it will appear, that most of those Nations which departed from *Babel* in a confusion, met in *Tyre* in such a
method as now inabled through industry, observation, and
entercourse, they could understand the languages and
traffick one with another.

* * * * * * * * *

Thus sate *Tyre* on her Throne in a Princely posture, no
less envious than proud : witness her rejoycing at the
destruction of *Jerusalem* (the breaking of one Merchant is
the making of another) when she said to her self, *Jerusalem
is turned unto me, I shall be replenished now she is made
wast* ; meaning that all trading divided before, should now
be engrossed to her self alone. But God marred her markets,
threatning by *Isaiah to stain the pride of her glory*, alluding
to *Tyres* master-piece which was to fix fair and fresh colours,
which God would soil and blur, notwithstanding all her
curiosity in that kind. *Ezekiel* useth two maritime expressions as most proper for a Port ; first that her enemies
should come up against her as *the Sea causeth his waves to
come up*, and then *that an East wind should break her*,
meaning that *Nebuchadnezzar* (living North-east from this
place) who afterwards besieged and sacked the City.

It seems the taking thereof, called elsewhere the strong City *Tyre*, did not quit cost for the taking thereof, the profit received by it not countervailing the pains expended upon it ; God himself confesseth that *Nebuchadnezzar served a great service against Tyre and yet had no wages*. One tells us that the *Tyrians* after thirteen years siege, despoiled of all hope of relief, abandoned their City, and in their ships transported their wives, children, and portable wealth to *Carthage*, *Cyprus*, and other Colonies, leaving *Nebuchadnez-* 10 *zar* their empty nest, when all the birds worth pluming, were flown away. However God afterwards gave him *the spoile of the Land of Egypt for wages for his Army*. Thus, not only those who do Gods will in a *direct line*, but also such, who collaterally (not to say casually) work his pleasure shall find a reward, seeing in sacking of *Tyre*, *Nebuchadnez-* *zar* went in the path and pace of his own pride and covetous- ness, though haply in his own way he met with Gods will not only besides his intention, but without the knowledge thereof.

20   As the ruines, so the restauration of *Tyre* was foretold by the Prophet ; not the same numericall *Tyre* in place and position (for *Paletyrus* or *old Tyre* ever after remained desolate according to the prediction, *thou shalt be built no more*) but the same in name, Country, convenience of site, wealth, and wickedness. Yea she exchanged and improved her place for commodity and strength, removing from the entrance to the midst of the Sea, from the continent to almost an Island. Here to use the Prophets expression after seventy years (the end of the *Babylonish* Kingdom) *Tyre* 30 began to sing as an harlot ; Siren songs to allure Merchants to be her lovers, as before ; counting trade and profit to be her richest pleasure. And so she did flourish again as much or more than ever, during the *Persian* Monarchy, about two hundred six years ; till *Alexander* the great made her change

her tune, alter her notes, and turn her merry love-songs into mournfull Elegies on her self. For being denied by the *Tyrians* in their City to sacrifice to *Hercules* the Tutelar God of that place, *Alexander* not so superstitious as ambitious, with vast pains and expence (as one whom no perill could affright, nor labour weary) sacked the City, putting such to the sword as resisted, and causing two thousand more to be hung up in rank on the Sea shore. At which time he built a Castle of his own name (now corruptly called *Sandalium*) two miles South of the City.   10

Yet *Tyre* afterwards recovered it self to considerable greatness, like a cunning Broaker, though often proving quite bankrupt, she set up again, though having nothing to give her credit but the conveniency of her situation : as indeed an harlot needs no other wares than her self to set up her trading. Insomuch that the Poets fiction of the *Phœnix* springing again out of his own ashes, being disclaimed by naturall History for a falshood, may mythologically find a truth in, and probably fetch its ground from this *Phœnix* or *Phœnician* City of *Tyre*, always arising fresh and 20 fair out of his own ruins. In our Saviours time it was a stately place, and yet though with *Dives* it was *clothed in Purple* ; *Tyre* could not with him *fare deliciously every day*, unless beholding to *Herods* land of *Galilee* to afford it constant provision, *because its Country was nourished by the Kings Country*. Sensible hereof when *Herod* was highly displeased with these of *Tyre* and *Sidon*, they politickly compounded the breach (knowing that to fight with him who fed them, was the ready way to be famished) and opening the breast of *Blastus* the Kings Chamberlain with 30 a golden key, through that passage they made their access to pacifie King *Herod*.

Tyre at this day is reduced almost to nothing. Here it is seasonably remembred that *Ethbaal* father of *Jezebel* was the King, as *Tyre* was the chief City of the *Sidonians*, and I find a great conformity betwixt the fortunes of his daughter and this place,

In their
1. Outward happiness. She a crowned Queen, and *Tyre* a *Crowning City*, whose Merchants were Princes.

2. Inward wickedness; both of them stiled Harlots in Scripture.

3. Finall wofulness; she eaten up by the dogs to the short reversion of her *skull*, *feet* and *palms*; and *Tyre* so consumed by all-devouring time, *that now no other than an heap of Ruines, yet have they a reverent respect*, and do instruct the pensive beholders with their exemplary frailty.

Enough of *Tyre*, if not too much : fearing that long since the Reader hath sadly sympathized with the sufferings of *Nebuchadnezzar* and *Alexander*, guessing their pains to be great in the long siege of this place by the proportion of their own patience in reading our tedious description thereof. All I will add is this, that though *Tyre* was a sink of sin, yet is this recorded in excuse of her profaneness, and mitigation of her punishment, that if *the miracles done in Chorazin and Bethsaida* had been done in *Tyre* and *Sidon*, they would have long since repented in sackcloth and ashes.

(Book ii. Ch. 5)

The Building of the Temple

Now *Solomon* his son being a peaceable Prince, as his name imports, in his quiet reign began the building of the Temple. Thus as Criers make an *O yes* to silence all noise, that men may the better attend to the Judge when beginning his Charge; so by a generall peace, *the rage of all people was stilled*, before God in the Oracle did begin his familiar discourse with the *Israelites*, or the foundation of the Temple taken in hand. Then *Solomon* enters on the work, emploiing in mount *Lebanon* a vast army of workmen, in their several distances to advance this Fabrick.

Namely, for servile work, an hundred and fifty thousand bearers of burdens, and hewers of stone and wood. All these were strangers, *Solomon* reserving his native subjects for their purses to pay taxes, not persons to bear burdens. Secondly, for plain work ; in which thirtie thousand *Israel-* ites were imployed, yet with such alternation, that, divided in three parts, they staied one month in mount *Lebanon*, and the other two at home. Thirdly, for carved-works ; herein the *Sidonians* only were used, whose exact number is not specified : But they must needs be numerous, if we may guess the men by their mouthes, and their mouthes by the proportion of victualls allowed them. Lastly, above all for direction three thousand three hundred were appointed (surely so many officers would suffer no drones to be in the whole hive) to oversee the rest.

Such who admire how so many could so long be busied in such a building, would haply have wondred more, how so few in so short a time could have finished the same, had they beheld the magnificence thereof. Two great gulfes there were, which insensibly swallowed up the labours of many thousands of men. First, the want of horses in *Judea* (plenty whereof were brought out of *Egypt* towards the latter end of King *Solomons* reign) whereupon massie timber in those mountainous countries, were managed by the main strength of men. The second was a religious Criticism peculiar to this structure, all things being before-hand so framed and fitted in Mount *Lebanon*, that *not so much as the sound of an Ax, or Hammer was heard in Jerusalem, when it came to be erected.* Which exactness must needs occasion many chargeable essays and samples, before it could be attained. Nor wanted there a mystery therein, because as the moving Tabernacle typified the *Church Militant*; so the Temple resembled the *Triumphant*, where those who shall be thought worthy to be admitted into glory, shall have nothing to do, but to be admitted into glory.

Some will say with *Nicodemus, How could these things be*, that no noise should be made at the erecting thereof? suppose but a bedstead having head, sides, feet, posts, 10 tester, cords, and curtains fitted before, it cannot be set up without some necessary noise. Yea grant their hammers or mallets cased with some soft matter, to bribe them to silence, yet they could not be made so mute, but that the very contusion and enforcement of the air, would unavoidably advance some sound. Nor were the beams of the Temple so far in love with their mortises, as to run into them, or the mortises so fond of the beams, as to embrace them of their own accord.

In answer hereto, some plead miracle, others exquisite 20 Art, and severall kinds of cementing, souldering, rivetting, screwing, glewing, and other devices unknown to our age. As for the *Rabbinicall* fancy, that *Solomon* with the bloud of the worm *Thamyr* effected this matter, most will account it improbable in it self, and unproportionable to Scripture. Others distinguish on the degrees of the noise; small in comparison of so great a work, and not obstreperous to a publick disturbance. But the best interpret it, that no laborious sound was heard from the hewing or squaring of Timber, or stone, but only a more chearfull, yea mellodious 30 harmony, from the happy conjunction, and compacting of parts together, now easily matched which had been contracted before. This I am sure, that what tongue-tied tools soever were used at the erecting of the Temple, too clamorous instruments were imployed at the destruction thereof,

*when they brake down the carved work thereof at once with
Axes and Hammers.*

Besides the two gulfes aforesaid, (the quick-sands of
many mens labours) it is also to be considered, that though
so wise a King as *Solomon* would not burden himself with
superfluous numbers, yet in this Fabrick, wherein he did
personate and represent the great God of Heaven, he consulted more with his magnificence, than his frugality, not
minding so much how many the building in bare necessity
did require, but how many the Builders with full authority
could command.

Notwithstanding so many labourers entertained in the
work, seven years was this Temple in building. Here some
will behold the sanctity and perfection of the *septenary
number*, so often occurring in Scripture, whilest we conceive
this the best reason, why just seven years were spent in the
building thereof, because it could not be ended in six,
nor accomplished within a shorter compass of time. Indeed
almost twice as much time (thirteen years) did *Solomon*
spend in building his own house : whereof this fair and
ingenious reason is rendered by *Josephus* ; *because he was
not so intent and earnest therein, as in the structure of the
Temple.* It is in another case reported to the praise of
*Boaz, the man will not be at rest, untill he have finished the
thing* ; so *Solomon*, during those seven years of the Temples
building, did not sleep in a cessation from, nor slumber in
an interruption of that work, which was intended for the
honour of God. Though in erecting his own Palace, as he
made it for his pleasure, so he did it at his leasure ; as
conveniencies would permit.

(Book iii. Ch. 2)

The Pyramids

To come now to the particular description of *Egypt*; *Nilus* flowing out of *Ethiopia*, compassed an Island called the *Isle of Dogs*; but, why so named, I know as little, as why those rich meadows lying betwixt *London* and *Black-wall*, are called after the same name, though better deserving to be termed the *Isle of Oxen*, from the fat cattel feeding therein. But, seeing no mention of this, or the next Island (which *Nilus* makes) in Scripture, we pass them by, confining our ensuing discourse to God's Word alone; save only, that
10 we will take leave to survey the Pyramids, because *Josephus* (though erroneously) conceiveth them built by the *Israelites*, when here living in bondage.

They stand not far from the western bank of the River, and are the younger brethren of the Tower of *Babel*, built (but with better success, because finished) on the same consideration, by the *Egyptian* Kings, *to make them a name*. Yet, who erected them Greeks agree ill with themselves, and worse with the *Arabian* Authors, so that *Pliny* gravely observes it a just punishment on the vanity of these
20 founders, that they are forgotten. Indeed, in the Criticisme of credit, the Artisans cunning might cry halfes in honour, with the Kings cost in this structure; but, both the one and the other are equally buried in silence, so that the most skilfull *Egyptian* Antiquary cannot out of these Hiero-glyphicks of Pomp and pride, read the name of either. Whilest the poor Midwives, who contrary to *Pharaohs* command, preserved the Hebrews children, are to this day remembred by their names, *Shiphrah* and *Puah*. Thus memories founded on the rock of vertue, stand firm and
30 fast; when they quickly fall, built on the foundered bottom of affected magnificence. Indeed, these Pyramids are of stupendious vastness, and may be termed *Arts Mountains*,

though mole-hills, yea, but warts, if compared to those which Nature had produced. So ridiculous is the unequall contest in point of bulk, betwixt their severall workmanships, that Natures Pismires may be said to exceed Arts Elephants.

Some to excuse the pride of these Builders, resolve their design on a point of policy, only to busie their people, to prevent in them laziness and luxury, (the mother of mutinies) knowing, so rich a Soile would invite them to riot, if out of employment. But (whatever was their principall secundary end intended such structures for sepulchres, where the builders Bodies lay, not interred, but immured, with all imaginable cost bestowed upon them. For, the *Egyptians* fondly conceived (Reader, pity them, and praise God that thou art better informed) that the Soul even after death, like a gratefull guest, dwelt in the body so long as the same was kept swept and garnished, but finally forsook it, and sought out a new body, if once the corps were either carelesly neglected, or dispightfully abused ; and therefore to woo the Soul to constant residence in their bodies (at least wise to give it no wilfull distaste, or cause of alienation) they were so prodigiously expensive both in Imbalming their dead, and erecting stately places for their monuments.

The long lasting of these Pyramids, is not the least of admiration belonging unto them. They were born the first, and do live the last, of all the *seven wonders in the world*. Strange, that in three thousand years and upwards, no avaritious Prince was found to destroy them, to make profit of their Marble, and rich materials ; no humerous, or spightfull Prince offered to overthrow them, meerly to get a greater name for his peevishness in confounding, than their pride in first founding them ; No Zelot-reformer (whilest *Egypt* was Christian) demolished them under the notion of Pagan monuments. But surviving such casualties, strange, that after so long continuance, they have not fallen like Copy-holds, into the hand of the Grand Signeur (as Lord of the Mannor) for want of repairing. Yea, at the present, they are rather ancient, than ruinous ; and, though weather-beaten in their tops, have lively looks under a gray head, likely to abide these many years in the same condition, as being too great for any throat to swallow whole, and too hard for any teeth to bite asunder.

(Book iv, Ch. 5)

ABEL REDEVIVUS:

OR

The dead yet fpeaking,

The Lives and Deaths of the
Moderne Divines.

1651.

The Death of Jerome of Prague

FROM the Counsell he was carried home to the Prison, and there for many dayes kept with bread and water, so that had the proudest Anchorite, pretending to the highest abstinence beene Commoner with him, it would have tired his swiftest Devotion to keepe pace with him ; much other hard usage he felt for the space of a twelve moneth, wherein *his feet were hurt in the Stocks, the Irons entered into his Soule.* So that long durance, short dyet, hard lodging, love of Life, hope of Libertie, feare of Torture, wanting friends to advise him, made such impressions upon him, that at last he was not onely contented to abjure all *Wickliefes* opinions for false, but also to allow the murder of his deare brother *Huss* to be a lawfull and laudible Act of exemplary Justice.

Here let none Tyrannically trample on the prostrate credit of a penitent sinner. Consider that he did not surrender the Castle of his integrity at the first summons, but kept it a full yeer, in many a furious assault, till the Constant battery of Importunity, made at last an unhappy

breach in his Soule. O there is more required to make a
man valiant, then onely to call an other Coward. Had we
beene in *Jeromes* Case, what we ought to have done we
know, but what we should have done God knowes. And
may we here remember the *Blessing* which *Jacob* bequeathed
as a legacie to one of his *Sonnes, Gad a Troope shall overcome
him, but he shall overcome at the last.* Let none looke to long
on the intermediate fals and failings to which the best
Saints of God, in this life, are Subject, but lift up their eyes
to the ultimate and finall victories of Gods servants, who at
last, through Christ, prove more then Conquerours.

But *Jeromes* Condition was rather impar'd then improu'd
by his recantation. Great is the Differance betwixt deliverance out of dangers of Gods giving in his due time, and
forcible escapes by sinister courses, which men rashly snatch
to themselves. The former is ever attended with inward joy
and quiet of Conscience, the Soule Solacing it selfe, not onely
in the end attained, but also in the lawfulnesse of the means
used therunto ; wheras when men doe not ishue out of a
danger by a doore of Gods opening unto them, but breake
through the wall, (as *Jerome* by perjury) by violent and
unwarrantable wayes, their minds are daily haunted with
scruples and perplexities, even sometimes to dolefull dis-
traction : besides, such escapes never grow prosperous,
rather easing then curing, and the comfort got by them
unraveleth againe, as it hapned in *Jerome* of *Prague.* By
whose objuration his conscience was wounded, God offended,
truth betrayed, good men made to grieve, and bad men to
insult, the malice of his Adversaries being no what abated in
violence, but increased in subtilty. For conceiving his recantation (as indeed it was) rather indited from his Tongue
then his Heart, these Spanels resolved to *Retrive the game,*
and to put him a fresh on the triall.

No fewer then 107 Articles were framed against him

and he brought to his purgation before the Councell. Here
the titular Patriarch of *Constantinople*, who formerly had
condemned *Huss* was appointed his judge ; Happy had
it beene, if this pragmaticall persecutor had had no more
power in *Constance*, then he received profit from *Constantinople*, whence he was onely qualified and dignified with an
Aeriall title. *Jerom* most valiently and eloquently assessed
the truth, recanting his recantation, and protesting that
nothing more troubled him in his life, then his former
cowardize. Thus, as the well levelled Canon, though at the
discharging by the force of the powder it recoyleth some
paces backward, yet it sendeth the Bullet to the right marke;
so *Jerom* now hit home, notwithstanding his former fearfull
failing, and became the more couragious in Gods cause : yea
bashfull blushing for their former faults, so becometh the
faces of good men, that it maketh them looke the more
beautifull.

Sentence of condemnation was presently passed upon him,
and a paper Miter was made for him to weare, wherein red
divels with monstrous visages were depainted, done to
affright the vulgar, who commonly carry their soules in
their eyes, much affected with such representations ; the
heathen Romans had a custome that at the Apotheosis, or
Pagan Canonizing of an *Emperor* for a god, when his body
was solemnly burned, an artificiall Eagle was curiously made
at the top of the Rogus or funerall pile ; and people perswaded, that that soaring Eagle did withall carry and con-
vey the *Emperors* soule into heaven : Or at leastwise was an
Embleme of his mounting up into happinesse. Thus this
pageant of painted divels was presented to the people to
possesse them with an opinion, that in the same sort the
Fiends of hell did arrest and seaze on the soule of *Jerom*, who
notwithstanding would have done well enough, if the divels
in flesh there present had not done more to him, then the

divels in paper. This Saint rather smiling at the folly then angry at the malice of his enemies, cheerfully put the Miter on his head ; *Did my Saviour, said he, weare a Crowne of thornes for me, and shall not I as willingly weare this foolish Cap for his sake ?*

He was fastened to the stacke, which was an image of wood made to resemble *John Huss* (sometimes deepe malice expresseth it selfe but in shallow fancies) and singing all the while, suffered (as I may say) many Marterdomes. It was
10 almost quarter of an houre, before he gave up the ghost, rather roasted then burnt : so as blisters, as big as Egs were raised upon his skin : the fire tormented him at distance, being made round about him. Here my soule being to be sent on two severall errands, knoweth not which first to dispatch : whether I should enveigh on the cruelty of his Murderers, who had martired all humanity in themselves, artificially skilfull to descant on the dolefull plain song of death, that the poore man might feele himself dye, whilest their revengefull eyes plaid the Epicures on his torment :
20 or shall I first admire the patience of *Jerom*, who standing as stiffe as the stake to which he was fastened, like *Eliah* went up to heaven in a Chariot of fire : But to omit both, I had best adore the goodnesse of God, which gave such strength unto men, conquering the cruelty of their tormentors by their sufferings.

The ashes of *Jerom* were cast into the river of *Rhine*, so that he might say with *David*, *We went through fire and water* : what the Poets fain of the river *Tagus* carrying golden sand in the streame thereof, is herein mistically
30 verified of *Rhine* ; now the chanell was enriched with the precious dust of this Saint : that river long since hath perchance scattered their reliques to the *German* sea, as that to the mayne Ocean, though his memory and fame is more dispersed abroad on the Continent. All this separation of

his dust shall not pose an omnipotent power, but that at the last day he shall have a glorious resurrection. Wicked men said of St. *Paul, Away with such a fellow from the Earth, for it is not fit that he should live.* God saith of his soule, *of whom the world was not worthy.* Both agree in this, though grounding their agreement on contrary wayes, that men of great piety are not to be long lived in this world.

The Life and Death of John Fox

John Fox was born at *Bosten* in *Lincolnshire Anno* 1517; his Parents were neither so rich as by their wealth to be exposed to envy, nor so meane as by want to be lyable to contempt; more enriched they were with the love of their Neighbours, and most of all in having this so towardly and hopefull a Son. These perceiving that nature pointed out their Son (by the rare parts bestowed upon him) to be a Scholar, and therefore following her directions carefully bred him in learning, and sent him to *Brazennose* Colledge in *Oxford.*

Here he was Chamber-fellow with *Alexander Nowell* afterwards Doctor and Dean of *Pauls,* and friendship betwixt them took so deep an impression in their tender years, advantaged with the simpathy of their natures, that it increased with their Age to be indelible. These communicated their studyes together, and with harmlesse emulation, and loving strife, whilest each endeavoured to out-strip others, both surpassed themselves.

Hence *Fox* was translated and chosen Fellow of *Maudlin* Colledge; whereat such as were bred in that foundation counting themselves the proper Heires to all the preferment in the House, were much offended, til his patience and humanity reconciled them unto him; so that he became not onely affected but admired. And as Naturalists observe that Plants are meliorated by removing, not abating their old but acquiring new spirits unto them ; so this Scholar by changing his Soyle to a new Colledge, was thereby marvelously improved in all manner of learning.

Now King *Henry* had lately set up a mongrell Religion in the Land, like the Toes of *Nabuchadnezars* image, partly Iron, partly Clay ; one moity thereof, strong with undeniable Truth, the other dawbed with untempered morter, in the six Popish Articles still retained. Our young Fellow in
10 the Colledge, sees and sighs at the superstition, and retiring himselfe to a grove, entertaines the time with Solitarinesse, onely the silent midnight was witnesse to his sobs and groanes. He sees what, but not whither to flye, but at last resolves hereafter to absent himselfe from the Romish Church : Hereupon being accused for a Separatist, and unwilling to overpurchase his safety at the price of a lye he is convented and expelled the Colledge. But because Theeves must be thanked for giving what they doe not take away, his enemies challenged Commendation due to their courtisie,
20 because they took not *Foxes* life from him, according to the Severity of the Laws then in force.

By this time his owne Father was dead and his Mother married againe ; *Fox* repaires to his Father in law for succour, but finds no entertainment. For as when a hunted Deere, chased with the Hounds, taketh sanctuary by flying to the rest of the herd, they out of a Principle of self preservation drive him away, for fear least the Hounds in persuit of him, fall on them ; so his *Father in law* was loath to receive him, and forbad him the protection of his family,
30 least Persecutors in quest of his Son should bring him and his whole houshold into trouble.

Here it would be tedious for us but to tell (and then how troublesome for him to endure) in how many places this poore man lurked, for fear of informers, those Birds of prey which have as quick sight as sharp Talons, sometimes at Sir *Thomas Luceys* in *Warwickshire*, sometimes at *Boston*, most commonly at *London*, taken covert in that forrest of houses ; it being a strange truth, that in such wherein are most eyes, a man is least seene. The *Foxes* (saith our Saviour) have holes, litterally true of that cunning creature, but our *Fox*, being indeed a sheep, in Innocence and Simplicity, had not where to lay his head, like Christ his Master.

But soone after hapned the death of King *Henry*, and *Edward* the sixt succeeded him. This put a period to his frights and flights, and for five years this good man enjoyed peace and prosperity, till the raigne of Queene *Mary* : Under whom for a while he lived safe in the house of the Duke of *Norfolke*, once his Pupill, untill *Gardner* Bishop of *Winchester*, that cruel Bloud-hound scenting him out, designed his destruction. For comming on a visit of respect to the Duke, *Fox* casually passing by, the Bishop demanded who that was ; my Physitian answered the Duke : the Bishop replyed, I like well his ingenuous countenance, and when I have need will make use of him. Thus *Herod* pretended he would worship Christ when he intended to kill him ; *Winchester* ment this Physitian should be his patient, on whom he would practice with fire and faggot, the usuall dosis prescribed to all those who were accused to be infected with the Protestant Religion.

Now flyes our *Fox* beyond the Seas, who escaping fire fell into as mercilesse an element of Water. A terrible Tempest overtook him, frighting the prophane Sea-men into their prayers, and melting their hearts, which might seeme made of those Rocks amongst which they sailed. Hereby he was driven back againe to *Yarmouth*, but at last by Gods Providence got beyond the Seas, and some months after arrived at *Basil*. Here he began that famous worke of Acts and Monuments, which he finished many years after : And here making a Sermon to his fellow Exiles, he plainly told them, *that now the Time was come for their returne into* England, *and that he brought them that newes by commandement from God.*

These Words were differently censured by severall men, some took them to be the evaporations of a melancholly Braine ; others as Words shot at random, which if casually hitting the marke, would afterwards be observed, if otherwise would be buried in *Oblivion* amongst a heap of other Expressions. A third condemned them for a presumptious intrusion into Gods secrets, prying into the Arke of future contingencies which God hath vailed onely for him : But the successe proved them to be Propheticall ; and this Confessour having his body macerated with fasting, and prayer and other afflictions, through the chinks and clefts thereof, stole a glympse of heaven and the knowledge of future things. For the day before his surrender, Queene *Mary* died ; and now *Fox* with the rest of his friends hasteth home, so that if feare gave them feet to runne beyond the Seas, joy gave them winges to flye home to their native Country.

Here arrived, he continued and finished that worthy Worke formerly begun. For as God preserved one of *Jobs* servants from fire and fury of the *Caldeans*, and *Sabeans*, to report to *Job* the losse of his fellowes ; so divine Providence protected this man from Martyrdome intended for him, that he might be the worlds intelligencer to tell the Tidings of the number and manner of Gods worthy Saints and servants who were destroyed by the cruelty of these Romish adversaries : Which bad newes is very well told in his Unpartiall relation.

For for the maine it is a worthy Worke (wherein the Reader may rather have then lack) presenting it selfe to Beholders, like *Ætna*, always burning whilst the smoke

hath almost put out the eyes of the adverse party, and these
Foxes fire-brands have brought much annoyance to the
Romish *Philistines*. But it were a Miracle if in so Voluminous a Worke there were nothing to be justly reproved ; so
great a Pomgranate not having any rotten kernell must
onely grow in Paradice. And though perchance he held the
beame at the best advantage for the Protestant party to
weigh downe, yet generally he is a true writer, and never
wilfully deceiveth, though he may sometimes be unwillingly
deceived. Many yeares after Master *Fox* lived in *England*, 10
highly favoured by persons of quality : So that it may seeme
strange, considering the heighth of his friends and largenesse
of his deserts, that he grew to no place of more honour,
and spread to no preferment of greater profit in the Church.
But this must be wholly imputed to his owne modesty in
declining advancement: For although the richest Myter
of *England* would have counted it selfe preferr'd by being
placed upon his head, yet he contented himselfe onely with
a Prebend of *Salisbury*, pleased with his owne obscurity,
whilst others of lesse desert make greater show. And whilest 20
proud people stretch out their Plumes in Ostentation, he
used their Vanity for his shelter, more pleased to have worth
then to have others take notice of it.

Now how learnedly he wrote, how constantly he preacht,
how piously he lived, how cheerefully he dyed, may be
fetcht from his life at large, prefixed before his book. One
passage therein omitted we must here insert, having received
it from witnesses beyond exception : In the eighty eight
when the *Spanish halfe Moone* did hope to rule all the motion
in our Seas, Master *Fox* was privately in his Chamber at 30
prayers, battering heaven with his importunity, in behalfe
of this sinfull Nation. And we may justly presume that his
devotion was as actually instrumental to the victory, as the
wisdom of our Admirable, valour of his Souldiers, skil and

industry of his Sea-men. On a sudden coming downe to his Family, he cryed out, *They are gone, they are gone* ; which indeed hapned in the same instant, as by exact Computation afterwards did appeare. . . .

He was not nipt in the Bud, nor blasted in the blossome, nor blowne downe when green, nor gathered when ripe; but even fell of his owne accord, when altogether whithered.

THE
CHURCH-HISTORY
OF
BRITAIN;

From the Birth of

JESUS CHRIST,

Untill the YEAR

M. DC. XLVIII.

ENDEAVOURED

By *THOMAS FULLER*

LONDON,

Printed for IOHN WILLIAMS at the signe of the Crown
in St. Paul's Church-yard, Anno 1655.

To the Reader

AN Ingenious Gentleman some Moneths *since in* Iest-earnest *advised me to make hast with my* History of the Church of England, *for fear (said he) lest the* Church of England be ended before the *History* thereof.

This History *is now, though* late (*all* Church-work *is slow*) *brought with much difficulty to an end.*

And blessed be God, the Church of England *is still, (and long may it* be) *in* being, *though* disturb'd, distempered, distracted, *God* help *and* heal *her most sad condition.*

10   *The* three first Books *of this Volume were* for the main *written in the Reign of the late King, as appeareth by the passages then proper for the Government. The other* nine Books *we made since* Monarchy *was turned into a* State.

May God alone have the Glory, and the ingenuous Reader the Benefit of my endeavours ; which is the heavy desire of

Thy Servant in *Iesus Christ*,

THOMAS FULLER.

From my chamber in
  Sion Colledge.

The British Tongue

20   Onely give me leave to insert a Line or two (some Pleasant Discourse will not do amiss, after so much Sad matter) in Commendation of the *British* Tongue, and Vindication thereof, against such as causelesly traduce it. First, their Language is Native. It was one of those which departed from *Babel* : and herein it relates to God, as the more immediate Authour thereof ; whereas most Tongues in *Europe* ow their Beginning to humane Depraving of some Original Language. Thus the *Italian*, *Spanish*, and *French*, Daughters, or Neeces to the *Latine*, are generated from the Cor-

ruption thereof. Secondly, Unmixed. For, though it hath
some few Forrain Words, and useth them sometimes ; yet
she rather accepteth them out of State, then borroweth
them out of Need, as having besides these, other Words
of her own to express the same things. Yea, the *Romans*
were so far from making the *Britans* to *do*, that they could
not make them to *speak* as they would have them : their
very Language never had a perfect Conquest in this Island.
Thirdly, Unaltered. Other Tongues are daily disguised with
forrain Words, so that in a Century of years, they grow 10
Strangers to themselves : as now an *English*-man needs an
Interpreter to understand *Chaucer*'s English. But the
British continues so constant to itself, that the Prophesies
of old *Teliessin* (who lived above a thousand years since)
are at this day intelligible in that Tongue. Lastly, Durable ;
which had it's Beginning at the Confusion of Tongues, and
is likely not to have it's Ending till the Dissolution of the
World.

Some indeed inveigh against it, as being hard to be pronounced, having a conflux of many Consonants, and some 20
of them double-sounded ; yea, whereas the Mouth is the
place wherein the *Office of Speech* is generally kept, the
British words must be uttered through the Throat. But this
rather argues the Antiquity thereof, herein running parallel
with the *Hebrew* (the common Tongue of the Old World,
before it was inclosed into severall Languages) and hath
much Affinity therewith, in joynting of words with Affixes,
and many other Correspondencies. Some also cavill, that
it grates and tortures the eares of Hearers with the Harsh-
nesse thereof : whereas indeed it is unpleasant onely to such 30
as are Ignorant of it. And thus every Tongue seems stam-
mering, which is not understood ; yea, *Greek* it self is Bar-
barisme to *Barbarians*. Besides, what is nick-named Harsh-
ness therein, maketh it indeed more full, stately, and mas-

culine. But such is the Epicurisme of Modern Times, to addulce all words to the Eare, that (as in the *French*) they melt out, in pronouncing, many essentiall Letters, taking out all the Bones, to make them bend the better in speaking : and such Hypocrites in their Words speak them not truly in their native Strength, as the plain-dealing *British* do, which pronounce every letter therein more manly, if lesse melodious. Lastly, some condemn it unjustly as a Worth-lesse Tongue, because leading to no matter of moment ; and, 10 who will care to carry about that Key, which can unlock no Treasure ? But this is false ; that Tongue affording Monu-ments of Antiquity, *some being left, though many be lost* ; and moe had been extant, but for want of Diligence in Seeking, and Carefulnesse in Preserving them.

(Book II. Cent. vii, 17, 18)

The Conversion of Edwin

Edwine, the King thereof, was Monarch of all *England*, with the Isles of *Man* and *Anglesey*, more puissant then any of His Predecessours. And this, saith *Bede*, was *In auspi-cium suscipiendæ Fidei, in good Handsell of the Faith* he was hereafter to receive. God first made him Great, and 20 after Gracious ; that so by his Power, he might be the more effectuall Instrument of his Glory. Now he had married *Edelburge*, daughter of *Ethelbert* King of *Kent* : to whom he not onely permitted free Exercise of Religion, to her self and her Servants, but also promised himself to embrace it, if, on Examination, it appeared the most Holy, and fittest for Divine Service. In the Court of this Queen was one *Paulinus*, a pious Bishop, who, with much Pains and little Profit, long laboured in vain to convert the Pagans. God hereby both humbling him, and shewing, that the Hour of 30 his Mercy shall not be ante-dated one Minute, by any humane Endeavours. However, *Paulinus*, seeing he could not be happy to gain, would be carefull to save ; and daily plyed the Word and Sacraments, thereby to corroborate his owne People in Piety.

Now it happened that one *Eumere*, a Swash-buckler (a Contemner of his own life, and thereby Master of another man's) sent from *Guichelm*, King of the *West-Saxons*, with an envenomed Dagger sought to kill King *Edwine* : when *Lilla*, one of his Guard, foreseeing the Blow, and interposing himself, shielded his Sovereign with his own Body, yea, 10 deaded the Stroak with his own Death. Loyalty's Martyr ; in a Case which is likely to find moe to commend, then imitate it, on the like occasion. *Edwine*, notwithstanding slightly hurt, was very sensible of the Deliverance, and promised, that if he might conquer the treacherous *West-Saxon* King, with his Adherents, he would become a Christian. And though there be no indenting, and conditional capitulating with God (who is to be taken on any terms) yet this in a Pagan was a good step to Heaven, and *Paulinus* was glad he had got him thus far ; especially, when in Earnest 20 of the Sincerity of his Resolution, he consigned over his infant-Daughter *Eansled*, to be baptized, whom *Paulinus* christened, with twelve moe of the Queen's Family. Well, the *West-Saxon* King was quickly overcome, and all his Complices either killed, or conquered, and yet King *Edwine* demurred to embrace Christianity. But he communicated with the sagest of his Counsell, with whom he had daily Debates, being loth rashly to rush on a matter of such Moment. And truly, that Religion which is rather suddenly *parched* up, then seasonably *ripened*, doth commonly *ungive* after- 30 wards. Yea, he would sit long alone, making company to himself, and silently arguing the Case in his own Heart, being partly convinced in his Judgement of the Goodnesse of the Christian Religion ; and yet he durst not entertain

Truth, a lawfull King, for fear to displease *Custome*, a cruell Tyrant.

Amongst the many Debates he had with his Counsell about altering his Religion, two Passages must not be forgotten ; whereof one was the Speech of *Coify*, the prime Pagan-Priest. *Surely* (said he) *these Gods, whom we worship, are not of any Power, or Efficacy in themselves ; for none hath served them more conscientiously then my self yet other men, lesse meriting of them, have received moe and greater Favours* 10 *from their hand, and prosper better in all things they undertake. Now, if these were Gods of any Activity, they would have been more beneficiall to me, who have been so observant of them.* Here the Reader will smile at *Coify* his Solecisme, wherein the Premisses are guilty of Pride, as the Inference thereon of Errour and Mistake. If he turn Christian on these termes, he will be taught a new Lesson : how not onely all outward things happen alike, to good and bad, *to him that sacrificeth, as to him that sacrificeth not* ; but also, that *Judgement beginneth at the house of God*, and the best men meet with 20 the worst Successe in Temporal matters. How ever, God was pleased to sanctifie this mans Errour, as introductory to his Conversion : and let none wonder, if the first *Glimmering* of Grace in Pagans, be scarce a degree above *Blindnesse*.

Better, in my opinion, was the plain Comparison, which another namelesse Courtier made at the same time. *Mans life* (said he) *O King, is like unto a little Sparrow, which, whilest your Majesty is feasting by the Fire in your Parlour with your royall Retinue, flies in at one Window, and out at* 30 *another. Indeed we see it that short time it remaineth in the House, and then is it well sheltred from Wind and Weather ; but presently it passeth from Cold to Cold, and whence it came, and whither it goes, we are altogether ignorant. Thus, we can give some account of our Soul, during it's abode in the Body,*

*whilest housed and harboured therein ; but where it was before,
and how it fareth after, is to us altogether unknown. If therefore* Paulinus *his Preaching will certainly inform us herein, he
deserveth, in my opinion, to be entertained.*

Long looked for comes at last. King *Edwine* almost three
yeares a *Candidate at large* of Christianity, cordially em-
braceth the same, and with many of his Nobles, and Multi-
tudes of his Subjects, is solemnly baptized by *Paulinus,*
in the little Church of St. *Peters* in *York,* hastily set up by
the King for that purpose, and afterward by him changed 10
into a firmer and fairer Fabrick. Thus, as those Children
which are backward of their Tongues, when attaining to
Speech, pronounce their words the more plainly and distinctly : so *Edwine,* long, yea tedious before his turning
to Christianity, more effectually at last embraced the same.
And when it was put to the Question, what Person most
proper to destroy the Heathen Altars ? *Coify* the chief
Priest tendered his Service, as fittest for the purpose,
solemnly to demolish what he had before so superstitiously
adored. Down go all the Pagan Altars, and Images at 20
God-mundingham (now *Godmanham,* a small Village in the
East-Riding of *Yorkshire*) and those Idols with their Hands
were so far from defending themselves, that their mock-
Mouths could not afford one word, to bemoan their finall
Destruction.

(Book II. Cent. vii. 39–43)

Venerable Bede

Now, although many in this Age posted from *England* to
Rome, possessed with an high opinion of the Holinesse
thereof ; yet sure I am, one of the best Judgement (namely
Venerable Bede) was often sent for by Pope *Sergius* himself,
to come to *Rome,* yet, for ought we can find, never went 30
thither : which, no doubt, he would not have declined, if

sensible of any transcendent Sanctity in that Place, to advantage the Dwellers therein the nearer to Heaven. This *Bede* was born in the Kingdome of *Northumberland*, at *Girwy* [now *Yarrow*] in the Bishoprick of *Durham*, brought up by St. *Cuthbert*, and was the profoundest Scholar in his Age, for Latine, Greek, Philosophy, History, Divinity, Mathematicks, Musick, and what not? Homilies of his making were read in his Life-time, in the Christian Churches; a Dignity afforded to him alone. We are much beholding to

10 his Ecclesiasticall History, written by him, and dedicated to *Ceolwoolfus* King of *Northumberland*. A worthy Work indeed, though, in some respect, we could heartily wish that his Faith had been lesse, and his Charity more. *Faith lesse*, in believing and reporting so many prodigious Miracles of the *Saxons*: except any will say, that this in him was not so much *Vitium Hominis*, as *Seculi*. *Charity more*, I mean to the *Britans*, being no Friend to them, and over-partial to his own Country-men; slightly, and slenderly touching *British* matters, onely thereof to make a *Pedestall*, the more

20 fairly to reare and advance his *Saxon* History thereupon.

Some report that *Bede* never went out of his Cell, but lived and died therein. If so, the Scholars of *Cambridge* will be very sory, because thereby deprived of their Honour, by *Bede*'s living once in their University; whose House they still shew, betwixt St. *John*'s Colledge and *Round-Church*, or St. *Sepulchres*. Surely *Bede* was not fixed to his Cell, *as the Cockle to his Shel*, seeing no Observance of his *Benedictine* Order imposed such a Penance upon him. Indeed his own words, in the end of his Book, give some Countenance to

30 their Conjecture of his voluntary Confinement, speaking of himself, *Cunctum tempus vitæ in ejusdem Monasterii habitatione peragens*. But his Expression imports onely his generall Residence therein, that he was no Gadder abroad, or Discontinuer from his Convent, for a long time; though he

might for some short space make his Abode elsewhere.
Thus, when of the Prophetesse it is said, *that she departed
not from the Temple* : we understand it not so, as if she never
went out thereof ; but that for the main, she spent the most
of her time therein.

He is generally surnamed *Venerable*, but why, Authours
differ therein. Some say, a Dunce-Monk, being to make his
Epitaph, was *non-pluss'd* to make that *Dactyle*, which is
onely of the *Quorum* in the Hexameter, and therefore at
Night left the Verse thus gaping,   10

> *Hic sunt in fossa* Bedæ ———— *ossa.*

till he had consulted with his Pillow, to fill up the *Hiatus*.
But returning in the morning, an Angel (we have often heard
of their Singing, see now of their Poetry) had filled up the
Chasma with *Venerabilis*. Others, disclaiming this Conceit,
assign this Reason : Because *Bede*'s Homilies were (as
aforesaid) read in all Churches in his Life-time ; *plain Bede*
was conceived too little, and St. *Bede* too much ; because,
according to Popish, (but not St. *Paul*'s) Principles, *Saint*
is too much Flattery to be given to any whilest alive ; 20
Solon allowing none *happy*, and this mine Authour none,
in this degree, *holy*, before their Death. Wherefore *Venerable* was found out as an Expedient to accommodate the
Difference, luckily hitting the Mark, as a Title neither too
high, nor too low ; just even to so good a man, and great
a Scholar, whilest alive. This is observable in all those who
have written the Life of *Bede* ; that, whereas such *Saxon-*
Saints, as had not the tenth of his Sanctity, nor hundredth
part of his Learning, are said to have wrought Miracles *ad
Lectoris nauseam* ; not one single Miracle is reported to 30
have been done by *Bede*. Whereof (under favour) I conceive
this the Reason : Monks, who wrote the Lives of many of
their Saints, knew little more of many of them then their
bare Names, and Times wherein they lived ; which made

them *Historiæ vacua miraculis supplere*, to plump up the Hollownesse of their History with improbable Miracles, swelling the Bowells of their Books with empty Wind, in default of sufficient solid Food to fill them. Whereas *Bede*'s Life affording plenty and variety of reall and effectuall Matter, the Writer thereof (why should a Rich man be a Thief, or Lyar ?) had no Temptation (I am sure no Need) to farse his book with fond Miracles, who might rather leave, then lack of materiall Passages therein.

10   One of the last things he did, was the translating of the Gospel of St. *John* into *English*. When Death seised on him, one of his devout Scholars, whom he used for his Secretary, or *Amanuensis*, complained, *My beloved Master, there remains yet one Sentence unwritten.* Write it then quickly, replied *Bede* : and summoning all his spirits together (like the last Blaze of a Candle going out) he indited it, and expired. Thus Gods Children are immortall, whiles their Father hath any thing for them to do on Earth ; and Death, *that Beast, cannot overcome and kill them, till first they have* 20 *finished their Testimony* : which done, like Silk-worms, they willingly die, when their Web is ended, and are comfortably entombed in their own Endeavours. Nor have I ought else to observe of *Bede*, save onely this ; A forreign Embassadour, some two hundred yeares since, coming to *Durham*, addressed himself first to the high and sumptuous Shrine of St. *Cuthbert, If thou beest a Saint, pray for me* : then coming to the plain, low, and little Tombe of *Bede, Because* (said he) *thou art a Saint, good* Bede, *pray for me.*

(Book II, Cent. viii. 15–18)

Chaucer

He was a great *Refiner*, and *Illuminer* of our English tongue (and, if he left it so bad, how much worse did he finde it ?) witness *Leland* thus praising him,

> *Prædicat Algerum meritò Florentia Dantem,*
> *Italia & numeros tota Petrarche tuos.*
> *Anglia Chaucerum veneratur nostra Poëtam,*
> *Cui veneres debet patria lingua suas.*

> Of *Alger Dants, Florence* doth justly boast,
> Of *Petrarch* brags all the Italian coast.
> *England* doth Poet *Chaucer* reverence,   10
> To whom our language owes its eloquence.

Indeed *Verstegan*, a learned Antiquary, condemns him, for spoiling the purity of the English tongue, by the mixture of so many French and Latin words. But, he who mingles wine with water, though he destroies the nature of water, improves the quality thereof.

I finde this *Chaucer* fined in the Temple two shillings, for striking a Franciscan Frier in *Fleet-street*, and it seems his hands ever after itched to be revenged, and have his penni-worths out of them, so *tickling* Religious-Orders with his 20 *tales*, and yet so *pinching* them with his *truths*, that Friers in reading his books, know not how to dispose their faces betwixt *crying* and *laughing*. He lies buried in the South-Isle of *St. Peters, Westminster*, and since hath got the company of *Spencer* and *Drayton* (a pair-royal of Poets) enough (almost) to make passengers feet to move metrically, who go over the place, where so much *Poetical dust* is interred.

(Book IV. Cent. xiv. 48, 49)

Richard III

Duke *Richard* was low in stature, crook-backed, with one shoulder higher then the other, having a prominent gobber-tooth, a war-like countenance which well enough became 30

a souldier. Yet a modern Author, in a book by him lately set forth, eveneth his shoulders, smootheth his back, planeth his teeth, maketh him in all points a comly, and beautiful person. Nor stoppeth he here, but proceeding from his naturals to his morals, maketh him as vertuous, as handsome (which in some sense may be allowed to be true) concealing most, denying some, defending others of his foulest facts, wherewith in all ages since he standeth charged on record. For mine own part, I confess it no heresie to maintain a
10 paradox in History, nor am I such an enemy to wit, as not to allow it leave harmlesly to disport it self for its own content, and the delight of others. Thus *Cardan* hath written his *Encomium Neronis*, and others (best husband-men who can improve the barrennest ground) have by art endeavoured to praise as improbable subjects. But, when men shall do it cordially, in sober sadness, to pervert peoples judgments, and therein go against all received Records, I say, singularly is the least fault can be laid to such mens charge. Besides, there are some Birds (Sea-pies by name)
20 who cannot rise except it be by flying against the winde, as some hope to atchieve their advancement, by being contrary, and paradoxal in judgment to all before them.

(Book IV. Cent. xv. Sect. iv, 8)

The Loss of Books at the Dissolution of Abbeys

The *English* Monks were bookish of themselves, and much inclined to hoord up monuments of learning. *Britain*, (we know) is styled *Another world*, and in this contradistinction (though incomparably lesse in quantity) acquits it self well in proportion of famous Writers, producing almost as many Classical School-men for her Natives, as all *Europe* besides. Other excellent Books of forraign Authors were brought
30 hither, purchased at dear rates ; if we consider that the

Presse (which now runs so incredibly fast) was in that Age in her infancie, newly able to goe alone, there being then few Printed Books, in comparison of the many Manuscripts. These, if carefully collected and methodically compiled, would have amounted to a Librarie, exceeding that of *Ptolomie*'s, for plenty ; or many *Vaticans*, for choicenesse, and rarity. Yea, had they been transported beyond the seas, sent over, and sold entire to such who knew their value, and would preserve them, *England*'s losse had been *Europe*'s gain, and the detriment the lesse to Learning in generall. Yea, many years after the *English* might have repurchased for pounds, what their Grand-fathers sold for fewer pence into forraign parts.

But alas ! those Abbeys were now sold to such Chap-men, in whom it was questionable, whether their *ignorance*, or *avarice* were greater, and they made havock, and destruction of all. As Broakers in *Long-lane*, when they buy an old suit, buy the lineings together with the out-side : so it was conceived meet, that such as purchased the buildings of Monasteries, should in the same grant have the Libraries (the stuffing thereof) conveyed unto them. And now these ignorant owners, so long as they might keep a *Lieger-book*, or *Terrier*, by direction thereof to finde such stragling acres as belonged unto them, they cared not to preserve any other Monuments. The covers of books, with curious brasse bosses, and claspes, intended to protect, proved to betray them, being the baits of covetousness. And so, many excellent Authors, stripp'd out of their cases, were left naked, to be burnt, or thrown away. Thus *Esop*'s cock, casually lighting on a pearl, preferr'd a grain before it ; yet he left it as he found it ; and, as he reaped no profit by the pearl, it received no damage by him. Whereas these cruell Cormorants, with their barbarous beaks, and greedy claws, rent, tore, and tatter'd these inestimable pieces of Antiquity.

Who would think, that the Fathers should be condemn'd to such servile employment, as to be Scavengers, to make clean the foulest sink in mens bodies ? Yea, which is worse, many an antient manuscript Bible cut in pieces, to cover filthy Pamphlets : so that a case of Diamond hath been made to keep dirt within it ; yea, the *Wisemen of Gotham*, bound up in the *Wisdome of Solomon*. . . .

What soul can be so frozen, as not to melt into anger hereat ? What heart, having the least spark of ingenuity, is
10 not hot at this indignity offered to literature ? I deny not, but that in this heap of Books there was much rubbish. Legions of lying *Legends*, good for nothing but fewell, whose keeping would have caused the losse of much pretious time, in reading them. I confesse also, there were many volumes full fraught with superstition, which notwithstanding might be useful to learned men ; except any will deny Apothe-caries the priviledge of keeping poison in their shops, when they can make antidotes of them. But besides these, what beautifull Bibles ? rare Fathers ? subtile School-men ?
20 usefull Historians, antient, middle, modern ? what painfull Comments were here amongst them ? what monuments of Mathematicks ? all massacred together ; seeing every book with a *crosse* was condemned for Popish ; with *circles*, for *conjuring*. Yea, I may say, that then holy *Divinity* was prophaned ; *Physick* it self, hurt ; and a trespasse, yea, a riot committed on the *Law* it self. And, more particularly, the History of former times, then, and there received a dangerous wound, whereof it halts at this day ; and without hope of a perfect cure, must go a cripple to the grave.

(Book VI. Sect. iv)

In praise of Bishop Jewell

30   A Jewell (sometimes taken for a single *precious stone*) is properly a *collective* of many, orderly set together to their

best advantage. So severall eminences met in this *Worthy man*. *Naturals*, *Artificials* (amongst which I recount his studied memory, deserving as well as *Theodectes* the *Sophister*, the *Sirname* of *Mnemonicus*) *Moralls*, but principally *Spiritualls*. So *devout* in the *Pew* where he *prayed*, *diligent* in the *Pulpit* where he *preached*, *grave* on the *Bench*, where he *assisted*, *milde* in the *Consistory* where he *judged*, *pleasant* at the *Table* where he *fed*, *patient* in the *bed* where he *died*, that well it were if in relation to him, *Secundum usum Sarum* were made *Precedentiall* to all *Posterity*. He gave at his death to *Peter Martyr a golden rose* (yet more fragrant for the *Worth* of the *Giver*, then the *value* of the *gift*) To the *City* of *Zurich* a *Present* which they converted into a piece of *Plate* with *Jewells Arms* thereon. To severall *Scholars*, large *Legacies*. To the *Church* of *Salisburie* a *fair Library*, and another to the *Church* of *England*, I mean his learned APOLOGIE. It is hard to say, whether his *soul*, or his *Ejaculations* arrived first in *Heaven*, seeing he prayed dying, and died praying. He was buried in the *Quire* by *Bishop Wivill*, Two *Champions* of the *Church* lying together, one who with his *sword* proffered to maintain the *Lands* ; The other, who with his *penn* defended the *Doctrine* thereof. In the absence of *Doctor Humfreys* designed for that service, Mr. *Giles Laurence* preached his *Funeralls*, who formerly (being *Tutor* to the *Children* of Sᵣ. *Arthur Darcy* by *Algate* in *London*) in *Queen Maries* dayes preserved *Jewells* life, and provided accommodation for his flight beyond the *Seas*.

(Book IX. Cent. xvi. Sect. iii, 2)

Hooker and Travers

Mr. *Hooker* his voice was low, stature little, gesture none at all, standing stone-still in the Pulpit, as if the posture of his body were the emblem of his minde, unmoveable in his

opinions. Where his eye was left fixed at the beginning, it
was found fixed at the end of his Sermon : In a word, the
doctrine he delivered, had nothing but it self to garnish it.
His stile was long and pithy, driving on a whole flock of
severall *Clauses* before he came to the *close* of a sentence.
So that when the copiousness of his stile, met not with
proportionable capacity in his auditors, it was unjustly
censured, for perplext, tedious, and obscure. His sermons
followed the inclination of his studies, and were for the most
part on controversies, and deep points of School Divinity.

Mr. *Travers* his utterance was gracefull, gesture plausible,
matter profitable, method plain, and his stile carried in it
indolem pietatis a Genius of grace flowing from his sanctified
heart. Some say, that the congregation in the Temple, *ebb'd
in the fore noon, and flowed in the afternoon,* and that the
auditory of Mr. *Travers* was far the more numerous, the
first occasion of emulation betwixt them. But such as
knew Mr. *Hooker,* knew him to be too wise to take exception
at such trifles, the rather because the most judicious is
always the least part in all auditories.

Here might one on Sundayes have seen, almost as many
writers as hearers. Not only young students, but even the
gravest *Benchers* (such as Sr. *Edw. Cook* and Sr. *James
Altham* then were) were not more exact in taking instruc-
tions from their clients, then in writing notes from the
mouths of their Ministers. The worst was, these two
preachers though joyned in affinity (their nearest kindred
being married together) acted with different principles, and
clashed one against another. So that what Mr. *Hooker*
delivered in the forenoon, Mr. *Travers* confuted in the afternoon. At the building of *Solomons* Temple 1 *King.* 6. 7.
neither hammer, nor axe, nor tool of iron was heard therein.
Whereas, alass in this *Temple,* not only much knocking was
heard, but (which was the worst) the nailes and pins, which

one masterbuilder drave in, were driven out by the other. To pass by lesser differences betwixt them about *Predestination*.

Hooker maintained.	*Travers* defended.
The Church of *Rome*, though not a pure and perfect, yet is a true Church, so that such who live and die therein upon their repentance of all their sins of ignorance may be saved.	The Church of *Rome* is no true Church at all, so that such as live and die therein, holding Justification in part by works, cannot be said by the Scriptures to be saved. 10

Thus much disturbance was caused to the disquieting of peoples consciences, the disgrace of the ordinance, the advantage of the common enemy, and the dishonour of God himself.

Here Arch-Bishop *Whitgift* interposed his power, and silenced *Travers* from preaching either in the Temple or any where else. It was lai'd to his charge : 1. That he was no lawfull ordained Minister according to the Church of *England*. 2ly. That he preached here without licence. 3ly. 20 That he had broken the order (made in the 7th year of her Majesties reign. Wherein it was provided, *that erroneous Doctrine, if it came to be publickly taught, should not be publicly refuted, but that notice thereof should be given to the Ordinary, to hear and determine such causes, to prevent publick disturbance.*

As for *Travers*, his silencing, many which were well pleased with the deed done, were offended at the manner of doing it. For all the Congregation on a Sabbath in the after noon were assembled together, their attention prepared, *the* 30 *Cloath* (as I may say) and napkins were laied, yea, the guests set, and their knives drawn for their spirituall repast, when suddenly as Mr. *Travers* was going up into the pulpit, a sorry

fellow served him with a letter, prohibiting him to preach
any more. In obedience to Authority, (the milde and constant submission whereunto won him respect with his
adversaries) Mr. *Travers* calmly signified the same to the
Congregation, and requested them quietly to depart to their
chambers. Thus was our good *Zacheus struck dumb in the
Temple*, but not for *infidelity*, unpartial people accounting
his fault at most but *indiscretion*. Mean time, his Auditory
(pained that their pregnant expectation to hear him preach,
10 should so publickly prove abortive, and sent sermonless
home) manifested in their variety of passion, some grieving,
some frowning, some murmuring, and the wisest sort, who
held their tongues, shaked their heads, as disliking the
managing of the matter.

(Book IX. Cent. xvi. Sect. vii. 53–57)

Godly Greenham

It may be said of some persons in reference to their
history, *that they were born men*, namely such of whose birth,
and youth, we finde no particular account. *Greenham* is
one of these, for, for want of better intelligence we finde him
full grown at the first, when *Anno Domini*, he was admitted
20 into *Pembroke Hall* in *Cambridge*. In which House some
years after, the youth of Mr. *Lancelot Andrews* (afterwards
Bishop of *Winchester*) was well acquainted with Mr. *Greenham* : and I dare boldly say, if *Greenham* gained any learning by *Andrews*, *Andrews* lost no religion by *Greenham*. He
afterwards left the University, and became Minister three
miles off at *Drie-Draiton*.

Drie-Draiton indeed, which though often watered with
Mr. *Greenhams* tears, and oftner with his prayers, and
preaching, moistened the rich with his counsel, the poor
30 with his charity, neither produced proportionable fruitful-
ness. The generality of his Parish remained ignorant, and

obstinate, to their Pastours great grief, and their own
greater damage and disgrace. Hence the Verses,

> *Greenham had pastures green,*
> *But sheep full lean.*

Thus God alone is the good shepheard, who doth feed, and
can fat his sheep, and can make them to thrive under his
keeping.

He used often, at the intreaty of some Doctors to preach
at St. *Maries* in *Cambridge,* where sometimes so great his
zeal in pressing important points, that he hath lost himself 10
in the driving home of some application, even to the for-
getting of his text (as himself would confess) till he recovered
the same on some short recollection. He alwayes bitterly
inveighed against Non-Residents ; professing, that he
wondered how such men could take any comfort in their
wealth. For, *me thinks* (saith he) *they should see written on
every thing which they have,* Pretium sanguinis, *this is the
price of blood.* But his master-piece was in comforting
wounded consciences. For, although *Heavens hand can only
set a broken heart,* yet God used him herein as an instrument 20
of good to many, who came to him with weeping eyes, and
went from him with chearefull souls. The breath of his
gracious counsel blew up much *smoking flax,* into a *blazing
flame.*

Hereupon the importunity of his friends (if herein they
proved so) perswaded him to leave his Parish, and remove
to *London,* where his publick parts might be better advantaged for the general good. They pleaded the little profit
of his long pains to so poore and peevish a Parish. Pitie
it was so good a fisher-man should cast his nets elsewhere, 30
than in that ocean of people. What was *Drie-Draiton* but
a bushel to hide, *London* an high candlestick to hold up the
brightness of his parts ? Over-intreated by others (even
almost against his own judgement) he resigned his Cure to

a worthy successour, and repaired to *London*. Where, after some years preaching up and down in no constant place, he was resident on no *Cure*, but the curing of consciences. I am credibly informed, he in some sort repented his removall from his Parish, and disliked his own erratical, and planetary life, which made him fix himself Preacher at last at *Christ-Church* in *London*, where he ended his dayes.

He lived Sermons, and was most precise in his conversation ; a strict observer of the *Lords-day*, and a great advancer thereof thorough the whole Realm, by that Treatise which he wrote of the Sabbath. No book in that age made greater impression on peoples practice, as one (then a great wit in the University, now a grave wisdome in our Church) hath ingeniously expressed.

On Mr. *Greenhams* book of the *Sabbath*

While *Greenham* writeth on the Sabbaths rest,
His soule enjoyes not, what his penn exprest :
His work enjoyes not what it self doth say,
For it shall never finde one resting day.
A thousand hands shall toss each page, and line,
Which shall be scanned by a thousand eine ;
That, *Sabbaths rest*, or this *Sabbaths unrest*,
Hard is to say whether's the happiest.

Thus godly *Greenham* is fallen asleep : we softly draw the curtains about him, and so proceed to other matter.

(Book IX. Cent. xvi. Sect. vii. 65-69)

Francis Bacon

None can character him to the life, save himself. He was *in parts*, more than a Man, who in any Liberal profession, might be, whatsoever he would himself. A great Honourer of *antient Authors*, yet a great Deviser and Practiser of new waies in Learning. Privy Counsellor, as to King JAMES, so to *Nature* it self, diving into many of her abstruse Mysteries.

New conclusions he would *dig out* with *mattocks* of *gold* and *silver*, not caring what his experience cost him, expending on the *Trials of Nature*, all and more than he got by the *Trials at the Barre*, Posterity being the better for his, though he the worse for his own, dear experiments. He and his Servants had *all in common*, the *Men* never wanting what their *Master* had, and thus what came *flowing* in unto him, was sent *flying* away from him, who, in giving of rewards knew no *bounds*, but the *bottome* of his own purse. Wherefore when King JAMES heard that he had given *Ten pounds* to an *under keeper*, by whom He had sent him a *Buck*, the KING said merrily, *I and He shall both die Beggars*, which was condemnable Prodigality in a *Subject*. He lived many years after, and in his Books will ever survive, in the reading whereof, modest Men commend him, in what they doe, condemn themselves, in what they doe not understand, as believing the fault in their own eyes, and not in the object.

(Book X. Cent. xvii. Sect. v. 22)

James I

He was of a *peaceable disposition*. Indeed, when he first entred *England*, at *Barwick*, He himself *gave fire to*, and *shot off* a *piece of Ordnance*, and that with good judgment. This was the onely *military act* personally performed by Him. So that He may have seemed in that *Cannon* to have *discharged Warre* out of *England*.

Coming to *Yorke*, He was somewhat amazed with the equipage of the *Northern Lords* repairing unto Him, (especially with the *Earl* of *Cumberland*'s) admiring there should be in *England* so *many Kings* ; for *less*, He could not conjecture them, such the *multitude* and *gallantry* of their *attendance*. But (following the counsel of His *English Secretary* there present) He soon found a way to abate the *formidable greatness* of the *English Nobility*, by conferring *Honour* upon many *persons*, whereby *Nobility* was spread so *broad*, that it became very *thin*, which much lessened the *antient esteem* thereof.

He was very eloquent in speech, whose *Latine* had *no fault*, but that it was *too good* for a *King*, whom *carelessness* (not *curiosity*) becomes in that kinde. His *Scotch tone* he rather affected than declin'd: and though His *speaking* spoil'd His *speech* in some *English ears*; yet the masculine worth of his *set Orations*, commanded *reverence*, if not *admiration* in all judicious hearers. But in common *speaking*, (as in His *hunting* he stood not on the *cleanest* but *nearest* way) He would never go about to make any expressions.

His *wit* was passing-sharp and piercing, equally pleased in *making* and *taking* a smart jest, *His Majestie* so much stooping to His *mirth*, that He never *refused* that *coine* which he *paid* to other folk. This made Him please Himself so much in the company of Count *Gondomer*: and some will say, the *King* was contented (for reasons best known to Himself) to be deceived by him, and humoured into a peace to His own disadvantage.

Once, King *James* in an Afternoon was praising the plentifull provision of *England*, especially for *flesh*, and *fowle*; adding, the like not to be had in all *Spaine*, what *one County* here did afford. Yea, but my *Master* (quoth *Gondomer*, there present) hath the *gold* and *silver* in the *East* and *West Indies*: And *I, by my Saule*, (saith the King) *have much adoe to keep my men from taking it away from Him*. To which the *Don's Spanish gravity* returned silence.

His *judgment* was most solid in matters of *Divinity*, not fathering Books of others, (as some of His *Predecessours*) but His *Works* are allowed His own by His very *adversaries*. Most *bountiful* to all, especially to *Scholars*, no *King* of *England* ever *doing* (though His *Successour suffered*) more, to preserve the *revenues* of the *English Hierarchy*. Most *mercifull* to *Offendors*, no one *person* of *Honour* (without parallel since the *Conquest*) being put to death in His Reign. In a word, He left His own Coffers *empty*, but His Subjects Chests *full*, the Land being never more *wealthy* ; it being easier then to *get*, than since to *save* an *estate*.

(Book X, Cent. xvii, Sect. vii, 27–32)

The Coronation of King Charles

The King entred at the West-gate of the Church, under a rich Canopy carried by the Barons of the *Cinque-Ports*, his own person being supported by Dr. *Neyle* Bishop of *Durham* on the one hand ; and Dr. *Lake*, Bishop of *Bath and Wells*, 10 on the other. His train being six yards long of purple Velvet, was held up by the Lord *Compton* (as belonging to the Robes) and the Lord *Viscount Dorcester*. Here he was met by the Prebends of *Westminster* (Bishop *Laud* supplying the Dean his place) in their rich Copes, who delivered into his Majesties hand the Staff of King *Edward* the Confessor, with which he walked up to the Scaffold.

This was made of wood at the upper end of the Church, from the Quire to the Altar. His Majesty mounted it, none under the degree of a Baron standing thereon, save only the 20 Prebends of *Westminster* who attended on the Altar, three Chaires were appointed for him in severall places ; one of *Repose*, the second the ancient *Chair* of *Coronation*, and the third (placed on an high square of five Staires ascent) being the Chair of State.

All being settled and reposed, the Lord Archbishop did present his Majesty to the Lords and Commons, East, West, North, South, asking their minds four severall times, if they did consent to the Coronation of King *Charles* their lawfull Soveraign. The King mean time presented himself bare- 30 headed : the consent being given four times with great acclamation, the King took his *Chaire* of repose.

After the Sermon (whereof before) the L. Archbishop, invested in a rich Coape, tendered to the King (kneeling down on cushions at the *Communion-Table*) a large Oath, then were his Majesties Robes taken off him, and were offered on the Altar. He stood for a while stripped to his Doublet and Hose, which were of white Satten (with Ribbons on the Armes and Shoulders, to open them) and he appeared 10 a proper Person to all that beheld him. Then was he led by the L. Archbishop and the Bishop of *St. Davids*, and placed in the *Chaire of Coronation* (a close Canopie being spread over him) the L. Archbishop anointing his head, shoulders, armes, and hands with a costly ointment, the Quire singing an Antheme of these words, *Zadok, the Priest anointed King Solomon.*

Hence the *King* was led up in his Doublet and Hose with a white *Coyfe* on his head to the Communion Table, where Bishop *Laud* (Deputy for the *Dean of Westminster*) brought 20 forth the ancient Habiliments of King *Edward the Confessour*, and put them upon him. Then was his Majestie brought back to the *Chaire of Coronation*, and received the Crown of King *Edward* (presented by Bishop *Laud*, and) put on his head by the Archbishop of *Canterburie*. The Quire singing an Antheme, *Thou shalt put a Crown of pure Gold upon his head*. Whereupon the *Earles* and *Viscounts* put on their Crimson Velvet Caps with Coronets about them (the *Barons* and *Bishops* alwayes standing bare headed) Then every *Bishop* came severally to his Majesty to bring 30 his *benediction* upon him, and he in King *Edwards* Robes with the Crown upon his head, rose from his Chaire, and did bow severally to every *Bishop* apart.

Then was *King Edwards Sword* girt about him, which he took off again and offered up at the Communion Table with *two Swords* more (surely not in relation to *Scotland* and *Ireland*, but to some ancient *Principalities* his Predecessors enjoyed in *France*). Then the *Duke* of *Buckingham* (as *Master* of the *Horse*) put on his *Spurres*, and thus completely crowned, his Majesty offered first *Gold*, then *Silver* at the *Altar*, and afterwards *Bread* and *Wine* which were to be used at the holy Communion.

Then was his Majesty conducted by the Nobility to the Throne upon that square Basis of five ascents, the Quire singing *Te deum*. Here his Majesty took an Oath of *homage* from the *Duke of Buckingham* (as *Lord high Constable* for that day) and the Duke did sweare all the Nobilitie besides to be *Homagers* to his Majestie at his Majesties knees.

Then as many *Earles* and *Barons* as could conveniently stand about the *Throne*, did lay their hands on the Crowne on his Majesties head, protesting to spend their bloods, to maintain it to him and his lawfull Heirs. The *Bishops* severally kneeled down, but took no oath as the Barons did, the King kissing every one of them.

Then the King took a Scrowle of parchment out of his bosom and gave it to the Lord Keeper *Williams*, who read it to the Commons four severall times, East, West, North and South. The effect whereof was, that his Majesty did offer a pardon to all his Subjects who would take it under his Broad-Seale.

From the Throne, his Majesty was conducted to the Communion Table, where the Lord Archbishop kneeling on the North side, read prayers in the Quire, and sung the Nicene Creed. The Bishop of *Landaff* and *Norwich*, read the Epistle and Gospell, with whom the Bishops of *Durham* and St. *Davids* in rich Copes kneeled with his Majesty and received the Communion; the bread, from the Archbishop, the wine, from the Bishop of St. *Davids*, his Majesty receiving last of all, whilest *Gloria in excelsis* was sung by the Quire, and some prayers read by the Archbishop concluded the solemnity.

The King after he had disrobed himself in King *Edwards* Chappell, came forth in a short Robe of red Velvet girt unto him, lined with Ermins, and a *Crown of his own* on his head set with very pretious stones, and thus the Train going to the Barges on the water side returned to *White Hall* in the same order wherein they came, about three a clocke in the afternoon.

10   I have insisted the longer on this Subject moved thereunto by this consideration, that if it be *the last* Solemnitie performed on an English King in this kinde, Posteritie will conceive my paines well bestowed, because *on the last.* But if hereafter Divine providence shall assign England another King, though the transactions herein be not wholly precedentiall, something of State may be chosen out gratefull for imitation.

(Book XI. Cent. xvii, Sect. i, 20–31)

Mr. John Dod

The same year with this *Arch-Bishop*, died another *Divine*, (though of a different judgement) no less esteemed
20 amongst men of his own perswasion, *viz.* Mr. *John Dod*, who (in the midst of troublesome times) quietly withdrew himself to heaven. He was born at *Shotledge* in *Cheshire* (the youngest of seventeen children) bred in *Jesus Colledge* in *Cambridge.* At a disputation at one Commencement he was so *facetiously solid* (*wild*, yet *sweet fruits* which the *stock* brought forth before *grafted* with *grace*) that *Oxfordmen* there present, courted him home with them, and would have planted him in their *University*, save that he declined it.

He was a *Passive Nonconformist*, not loving any one the
30 *worse* for difference in judgement about *Ceremonies*, but all the *better* for their unity of affections in *grace* and *good-*

ness. He used to retrench some hot spirits when enveighing against *Bishops,* telling them how *God* under that government had given a marvelous increase to the Gospell, and that godly men might comfortably comport therewith, under which *learning* and *religion* had so manifest an *Improvement.* He was a good *Decalogist,* and is conceived to his dying day (how roughly soever used by the opposite party) to stick to his own judgement of what he had written on the *fifth Commandement,* of *Obedience to Lawful Authority.*

Some *riotous Gentlemen* casually coming to the table of Sr. *Anthony Cope* in *Hanwell* were *half-starved* in the midst of a *feast,* because refraining from *swearing* (*meat* and *drink* to them) in the presence of Mr. *Dod*; of these *one* after dinner ingeniously professed, that he thought it had been impossible for himself to forbear *oaths* so long a time. Hereat Mr. *Dod* (the *flame* of whose *zeal* turned all accidents into *fuel*) fell into a pertinent and seasonable discourse (as more better at *occasionals,*) of what power men have more then they know of themselves to refrain from sin, and how active Gods restraining grace would be in us to bridle us from wickedness, were we not wanting to our selves.

Being striken in years, he used to compare himself to *Sampson* when his hair was cut off. I rise saith he in a morning as *Sampson* did, and think, *I will go out as at other times, goe, watch, walk, work, studie, ride, as when a young man; But alass he quickly found an alteration, and so do I, who must stoop to age, which hath clipt my hair and taken my strength away.*

Being at *Holdenbie,* and invited by an *Honourable person* to see that stately house built by Sr. *Christopher Hatton,* (the Masterpiece of English Architecture in that age) he desired to be excused, and to sit still looking on a *flower* which he had in his hand. *In this Flower* (saith he) *I can see more of God, then in all the beautiful buildings in the world.* And at this day as his *flower* is long since *withered*, That magnificent *Pile* (that *fair flower* of *art*) is altogether *blasted* and *destroyed*.

It is reported, he was but coursly used of the *Cavaliers*, who (they say) plundered him of his linnen and household-stuff, though (as some tell me) if so disposed, he might have redeemed all for a very small matter. However the good man still remembred his old maxime, *Sanctified afflictions are good Promotions*, and I have been credibly informed, that when the souldiers brought down his sheets out of the Chamber, into the room where Mr. *Dod* sate by the fire side ; He (in their absence to search after more) took one pair and clapt them under his Cushion whereon he sat, much pleasing himself after their departure that he had (as he said) *plundred the plunderers*, and by a *lawfull felony* saved so much of his own to himself.

He was an excellent scholer, and was as causlessly accused, as another *John*, of his name (Mr. *John Fox* I mean) for *lacking of latin*. He was also an exquisite *Hebrician*, and with his society and directions in one Vacation taught that tongue unto Mr. *John Gregorie* that rare Linguist, and Chaplain of *Christs-Church*, who survived him but one year, and now they both together praise God in that language, which glorified *Saints* and *Angels* use in heaven.

He was buried at *Fausly* in *Northampton*-shire, with whom the *Old Puritan* may seem to expire, and in his grave to be interr'd. Humble, Meek, Patient, Hospital, Charitable as in his censures of, so in his alms to others. Would I could truly say but half so much of the next Generation.

(Book XI. Cent. xvii, Sect. ix (= v). 85–92)

The Burial of King Charles

On the *Wednesday* sennight after, His Corpse embalmed, and coffined in lead, was delivered to the care of two of His servants, to be buried at *Windsor*. The one *Anthony Mildmay*, who formerly had been His *Sewer*, as I take it : the other *John Joyner*, bred first in His Majesties Kitchin, afterwards a Parliament-Captain, since by them deputed (when the *Scots* surrendred His person) Cook to His Majesty. This night they brought the Corpse to *Windsor*, and digged a grave for it in *S. George* his Chappel, on the South side of the Communion-Table. 10

But next day the Duke of *Richmond*, the Marquess of *Hertford*, the Earles of *South-Hampton*, and *Lindsey* (others, though sent to, declining the service, so far was their feare above their gratitude to their dead Master) came to *Windsor* and brought with them two Votes, passed that morning in Parliament ; Wherein the ordering of the Kings buriall, for the form and manner thereof, was wholy committed to the Duke of *Richmond*, provided, that the expence thereof exceeded not five hundred pounds. Coming into the Castle, they shewed their Commission to the Governor Colonel 20 *Wichcot*, desiring to interr the Corpse, according to the Common-Prayer-Book of the Church of *England*. The rather, because the Parliaments total remitting the manner of the Buriall to the Dukes discretion, implied a permission thereof. This the governor refused, alledging, it was improbable that the Parliament would permit the use of what so solemnly they had abolished, and therein destroy their own Act.

The Lords returned, that there was a difference betwixt *destroying* their own act, and *dispensing* with it, or *suspend-* 30 *ing* the exercise thereof. That no power so bindeth up its own hands, as to disable it self in some cases, to recede from the rigour of their own acts, if they should see just occasion. All would not prevaile, the Governour persisting in the negative, and the Lords betook themselves to their sad employment.

They resolved not to interre the Corpse in the grave which was provided for it, but in a Vault, if the Chappel afforded any. Then fall they a searching, and in vain seek for one in King *Henry* the eighth His Chappel (where the tombe, intended for Him by Cardinal *Wolsey*, lately stood) because all there was solid earth. Besides, this place at the present, used for a Magazine, was unsuiting with a solemn sepulture. Then with their feet they tried the Quire, to see if a sound would confess any hollowness therein, and at last (directed by one of the aged *poore Knights*) did light on a Vault in the middle thereof.

It was altogether darke (as made in the middest of the Quire) and an ordinary man could not stand therein without stooping, as not past five foot high. In the midst thereof lay a large leaden coffin (with the feet towards the *East*) and a far less on the left side thereof. On the other side was room, neither to spare nor to want, for any other coffin of a moderate proportion.

That one of the Order was buried there, plainly appeared by perfect pieces of purple-velvet, (their proper habit) remaining therein. Though some pieces of the same velvet were fox-tawnie, and some cole-black (all eye of purple being put out therein,) though all originally of the same cloath, varying the colour, as it met with more, or less moisture, as it lay in the ground.

Now a concurrence of presumptions concluded this great Coffin to contain the Corpse of King *Henry* the eighth, though there was neither Armes, nor any inscription to evidence the same.

1. The place exactly corresponds to the designation of His burial, mentioned in His last Will and Testament.

2. The small Coffin, in all probability was His Queens, *Jane Semaurs* (by whom in His Will He desired to be buried) and the room on the other side seems reserved, for His surviving Wife, Queen *Katherine Parr*.

3. It was never remembred, nor recorded, that any Subject of that Order, was interred in the body of that Quire, but in by-Chappels.

4. An herse stood over this vault, in the dayes of Queen *Elizabeth*, which (because cumbering the passage) was removed in the reign of King *James*.

I know a tradition is whispered from mouth to mouth, that King *Henry* His body was taken up, and burned in the reign of Queen *Mary*, and could name the Knight (Her Privie-Councellor, and then dwelling not far off) muttered to be employed in this inhumane action. This prevailed so far on the Lord *Herberts* belief, that he closeth his History of King *Henry* the eighth, with these suspicious words. *To conclude, I wish I could leave Him in His grave*. But there is no certainty hereof, and more probable that here He quietly was reposed. The lead-coffin, being very thin was at this time casually broken, and some yellow stuff, altogether sentless, like powder of gold, taken out of it (conceived some exsiccative gumms wherewith He was embalmed) which the Duke caused to be put in again, and the Coffin closed up.

The Vault thus prepared, a scarfe of lead was provided some two foot long, and five inches broad, therein to make an inscription. The Letters the Duke himself did delineate, and then a workman call'd to cut them out with a Chesil. It bare some debate, whether the letters should be made in those *concavities* to be cut out, or in the *solid lead* betwixt them. The latter was concluded on, because such vacuities are subject to be soon filled up with dust, and render the inscription legible, which was

KING CHARLES 1648.

The Plummer souldred it to the Coffin, about the brest of the Corpse, within the same.

All things thus in readiness, the Corpse was brought to the vault, being borne by the souldiers of the Garrison. Over it *a black velvet herse-cloth*, the foure labels whereof the foure Lords did support. The Bishop of *London* stood
10 weeping by, to tender that his service which might not be accepted. Then was It deposited in silence and sorrow, in the vacant place in the vault (the herse-cloth being cast in after it) about three of the clock in the afternoone ; and the Lords that night (though late) returned to *London*.

(Book XI. Conclusion)

THE APPEAL

OF

Injured Innocence.

CHAP. XII.

That the Author Designed unto himself no Party-pleasing *in Writing his* Church-History.

PARTIALITY is constantly charged on me by the *Anim-advertor*, and once, *with a witness*, as followeth, *pag.* 257.

> *We see by this, as by like Passages, which way our Author's Bowle is BYASSED, how constantly he declares himself in Favour of those who have either Seperated from the Church, or appeared against it.*

I *return*, (to prosecute his *Metaphor*) that I have used as *UPRIGHT BOWLES* as ever any that enter the *Alley* of 10 *History*, since our *Civil Dissentions*.

I do freely declare my self, that I in *Writing* my *Book*, am for the *Church* of *England*, as it stood established by Law ; the *Creed* being the *Contracted Articles*, and the 39 *Articles* the *Expanded Creed* of her *Doctrine*, as the *Canons* of her *Discipline*. And still I prise her *Favour* highest, though for the present it be least worth, as *little able* to *protect*, and *less* to *prefer* any that are faithfull to her *Interest*.

As for *pleasing* of *Parties*, I never *Designed* or *Endevoured* it. There were a kind of *Philosophers*, called *ELECTICI*, 20 which were of *none*, yet of *all Sects*, and who would not *engage in gross* in the *Opinions* of any *Philosophers*, but did *pick* and *choose* here and there, what they found *Consonant* to *Truth*, either amongst the *Stoicks*, *Peripatèticks*, *Academicks*, or (misinterpreted *Epicures*,) *receiving* that, and *rejecting* the rest ; such my *Project* to *commend* in all *Parties* what I find *praise-worthy*, and *condemne* the *rest* ; on which Account, some *Fleer*, some *Frown*, none *Smile* upon me.

First, for the *Papists*, though I malice not their *Persons*, and have a *Pity* (as *God* I hope hath a *Mercy*) for many
10 amongst them, yet I do, as *occasion* is offered, dislike their *Errors*, whereby I have incurred (and according to their *principles*) deserved their *Displeasure*.

The old *Non-conformists* being the same with the modern *Presbuterians*, but *depressed and under*, as the modern *Presbuterians* are the old *Non-conformists*, but *vertical* and in *Authority*, do (though the *Animadvertor* twitteth me constantly to Advocate for them) take great and general exception at me ; and it is not long since, in a Meeting of the most Eminent amongst them, I was told, that *I put too much Gall*
20 *into my Inck against them*.

The *Independent*, being the *Benjamin* of Parties, (and his *Mess* I assure you is none of the least) taxeth me for too much fieriness, as the *Animadvertor* (in his Expression lately cited) chargeth me for too much Favour unto them.

Thomas Lord *Coventry*, when coming from the *Chancery* to sit down at *Dinner*, was wont to say, *Surely, to day I have dealt equally, for I have displeased both sides*. I hope that I have his *Happiness*, for I am sure I have his *Unhappiness*, that having disobliged all Parties, I have written the very
30 Truth. Thus I can onely privately comfort my self in my owne Innocence, and hope that when my Head is laid low, what seems *too sweet, too bitter, too salt, too fresh* to the *present divided Age*, will be adjudged *well tasted* and *seasoned* to the Palate of *Unpartial Posterity*.

CHAP. XIII

What Good *the* Animadvertor *might, but would
not doe ; and, what* Good, *by Gods goodness
he Herein hath done unto the* Author.

When the *Animadvertor* had perused my *Book*, marking
some (but making moe) faults therein, it was in his Power
to have done me a Pleasure, the greatest he could give, or
I receive, *viz.* not to *paradigmatize* me, but by Letter in an
amicable way to impart my Mistakes unto me, that I might
amend them in my next *Edition*. Say not, He owed me no
such thing, who would have beheld it not as a *Debt* paid 10
unto, but *Alms* bestowed upon me.

I was not wholly without hope hereof, having found
such favour from some worthy Friends. Had the *Animadvertor* done the like, How had he obliged me ? As the
Society of *Peter-house* do preserve the Pictures of their
Benefactors in their Parlour, so would I have erected unto
him a Monument of Gratitude in my Heart, besides my
publick acknowledgement of the courtesie.

But it seems He intended not my Information, but De-
famation. However, he hath done to me a great good turn, 20
for which (because not intended) I will thank *God, viz.* He
by his causeless Carping hath allayed in me the delight
in Writing of *Histories* ; seeing nothing can be so unpartially
and inoffensively written, but some will carp thereat.

Mothers minding to wean their Children, use to put Soot,
Wormwood or Mustard on the Nibbles of their Breasts. God
foresaw I might Suck to a Surfet in Writing *Histories*, which
hath been a Thief in the Lamp of my Life, wasting much
Oyle thereof. My Head and Hand had robb'd my Heart in
such delightful Studdies. Wherefore he raised the bitter Pen 30
of the *Animadvertor* to wean me from such Digressions from
my Vocation.

I now experimentally find the Truth of *Solomon*'s words, *Of making many Books there is no End*. Not, but that all *perfect Books* (I mean *perfect* in *sheets*, otherwise none save Scripture *perfect*) have *Finis* in the Close thereof ; or that any Author is so irrational, but He propounds an End to himself before he begins it ; but that in *making of many Books there is no end* ; that is, the Writers of them seldom or never do attain that End which they propound to themselves, especially if Squinting at sinister Ends, as who is not *flesh* and *blood* ? Such as project wealth to themselves, are commonly by unwise managing, or casual miscarriage, impaired thereby in their Estates. Others who designed to themselves, (with the *builders* of *Babel*) to *get them a Name*, commonly meet with shame and disgrace. Or else, when their Books *are ended*, yet they are *not ended*, because though never so cautiously written, some Antagonists will take up the Bucklers against them, so that they must *begin* again after they have *ended*, (or sink in their credits) to write in their own vindication, which is my case, enough to take *off my edge*, formerly *too keen* in making multiplicity of Books.

I confess, I have yet one *History* ready for the Press, which I hope will be for Gods Glory and Honour of our Nation. This new-built Ship is now on the *Stocks*, ready to be lanched ; and being a Vessel of *great Burden*, God send me some good Adventurers to bear part of the Expence. This done, I will never meddle more with making any Books of this Nature. It is a provident way, before *Writing leave us*, to *leave of Writing* ; and the rather, because *Scribling* is the *Frequentative* thereof.

If therefore my *Petitioning* and *Optative* Amen, shall meet with Gods *Commissioning* and *Imperative* Amen, I will hereafter totally attend the Concernments of my Calling, and what directly and immediately shall tend to the advance of

Devotion in my self and in Others, as preparatory to my Dissolution out of this state of Mortality.

To my Loving Friend, Doctor *Peter Heylyn*.

I *hope, Sir, that we are not mutually Un-friended by this Difference which hath happened betwixt us. And now, as Duellers, when they are* Both out of breath, *may stand still and Parley, before they have a* Second passe, *let us in cold Blood exchange a Word, and, mean time, let us depose, at least suspend, our Animosities.*

Death hath crept into both our Clay-Cottages *through the* 10 Windows ; *your* Eyes *being* Bad, *mine* not Good, *God mend them both. And Sanctifie unto us these* Monitors *of* Mortality, *and however it fareth with our* Corporeall sight, *send our Souls that* Collyrium, *and* Heavenly Eye-salve, *mentioned in Scripture. But indeed Sir, I conceive our* Time, Pains, *and* Parts, *may be better expended to Gods Glory, and the Churches Good, than in these needlesse Contentions. Why should* Peter *fall out with* Thomas, *both being Disciples to the same Lord and Master. I assure you, Sir, (whatever you conceive to the contrary) I am Cordiall to the cause of the* English Church, 20 *and my Hoary Haires will go down to the Grave in sorrow for her Sufferings.*

You well remember the passage in Homer, *how* wise Nestor *bemoaned the unhappy difference betwixt* Agamemnon *and* Achilles.

> ῏Ω πόποι, ἦ μέγα πένθος ᾿Αχαΐδα γαῖαν ἱκάνει,
> ῏Η κεν γηθήσαι Πρίαμος, Πριάμοιό τε παῖδες,
> ῎Αλλοι τε Τρῶες μέγα κεν κεχαροίατο θυμῷ
> Εἰ σφῶιν τάδε πάντα πυθοίατο μαρναμένοῦν.

O gods ! how great the grief of *Greece* the while,　　　30
And *Priams* selfe, and Sons do sweetly smile,
Yea all the Trojan party swell with Laughter,
That Greeks with Greeks fall out, and fight to Slaughter.

Let me therefore tender unto you an Expedient in Tendency to our mutuall Agreement. You know full well Sir, *how in* Heraldry, two Lioncells Rampant endorsed, *are said to be the* Embleme *of two* Valiant Men, *keeping* appointment *and meeting in the* Field, *but, either forbidden fight by their* Prince, *or departing on Tearms of Equallity agreed betwixt themselves. Whereupon turning* Back to Back, *neither* Conquerors *nor* Conquered, *they depart the Field severall wayes, (their Stout Stomacks not suffering them both to go the same way) lest it* be accounted an Injury, one to precede the other.

In like manner, I know you disdain to allow me your Equall *in this* Controversie *betwixt us, and I will not allow you my* Superiour. *To prevent future Trouble, let it be a* Drawn Battle, *and let both of us* abound in our owne sense, *severally perswaded in the Truth of what we have written. Thus,* parting *and going out* Back *to* Back *here, (to cut off all Contest about* Precedency), *I hope we shall* meet *in* Heaven, Face to Face, *hereafter. In Order whereunto, God willing, I will give you a meeting, when, and where, you shall be pleased to appoint,* that we, who have Tilted Pens, *may* shake Hands *together.*

St. Paul *writing to* Philemon *concerning* Onesimus, *saith,* For perhaps he therefore departed for a season, that thou mightest receive him for ever. *To avoid exceptions, you shall be the good* Philemon, *I the fugitive* Onesimus. *Who knoweth but that God in his providence permitted, yea ordered this difference to happen betwixt us ; not onely to occasion a reconciliation, but to consolidate a mutuall friendship betwixt us, during our Lives ; and that the surviver (in Gods pleasure onely to appoint) may make favourable and respectfull mention* of him, who goeth first to his grave. *The desire of him who* remaines,

SIR,

A Lover of your Parts, and an Honourer of your Person,

THO. FULLER.

THE
HISTORY
OF THE
WORTHIÉS
OF
ENGLAND.

Endeavoured by
Thomas Fuller, D.D.

LONDON,
Printed by *J.G.W.L.* and *W.G.* MDCLXII.

The design of the ensuing work

ENGLAND may not unfitly be compared to an House not *very great*, but *convenient*, and the several Shires may properly be resembled to the *rooms* thereof. Now, as learned Master *Camden* and painful Master *Speed* with others, have discribed the *rooms* themselves ; so is it our intention, God willing to discribe the *Furniture* of those *rooms* ; such Eminent Commodities, which every County doth produce, with the Persons of Quality bred therein, and some other observables coincident with the same subject.

10   *Cato* that great and grave Philosopher did commonly demand, when any new Project was propounded unto him, *Cui Bono, what good would ensue, in case the same was effected.* A Question more fit to be *asked*, then facile to be *answered* in all undertakings, especially in the setting forth *of new Books*, Insomuch, that they themselves, who complain, That *They are too many already*, help dayly to make them more.

Know then, I propound *five ends* to my self in this Book : First, *To gain some Glory to God.* Secondly, *To preserve the* 20 *Memories of the Dead.* Thirdly, *To present Examples to the Living.* Fourthly, *To entertain the Reader with Delight.* And lastly, (which I am not ashamed publickly to profess) *To procure some honest profit to my self.* If not so happy to obtain all, I will be joyful to attain some, yea, contented and thankful too, if gaining any [especially the *First*] of these Ends, the Motives of my Endeavours.

First, *Glory to God*, which ought to be the aim of all our actions, though too often our bow starts, our hand shakes, and so our arrow misseth the mark. Yet I hope that our 30 discribing so good a Land, with the various Fruits and fruitful varieties therein, will ingage both Writer and Reader, in gratitude to that God, who hath been so bountiful to our Nation. In order whereunto, I have not only alwayes taken, but often sought occasions, to exhort to thankfulness ; hoping the same will be interpreted, no *stragling from my Subject*, but *a closing with my Calling*.

Secondly, *To preserve the Memories of the Dead*. A good name is an oyntment poured out, smelt where it is not seen. It hath been the lawful desire of men in all ages to perpetuate their Memories, thereby in some sort revenging themselves of Mortality, though few have found out effectual means to perform it. For Monuments made of 10 Wood, are subject to be burnt ; of Glass, to be broken ; of soft stone, to moulder ; of Marble and Metal, (if escaping the teeth of Time) to be demolished by the hand of Covetousness ; so that in my apprehension, the safest way to secure a memory from oblivion, is (next his own Vertues) by committing the same in writing to Posterity.

Thirdly, *To present examples to the living*, having here precedents of all sorts and sizes ; of men famous for *Valour*, *Wealth, Wisedome, Learning, Religion, and Bounty to the publick*, on which last we most largely insist. The Scholar 20 being taxed by his Writing-Master, for idlenesse in his absence, made a fair defence, when pleading that his Master had neither left him *Paper* whereon, or *Copy* whereby to write. But rich men will be *without excuse*, if not expressing their bounty in some proportion, God having provided them *Paper* enough, [*The poor you have alwayes with you*] and set them *signal examples*, as in our ensuing Work will plainly appear.

Fourthly, *To entertain the Reader with delight*. I confess the subject is but dull in it self, to tell the time and place 30 of mens birth, and deaths, their names, with the names and number of their books, and therefore this bare Sceleton of *Time, Place*, and *Person*, must be fleshed with some pleasant passages. To this intent I have purposely inter-

laced (not as meat, but as condiment) many delightful
stories, that so the Reader if he do not arise (which I hope
and desire) *Religiosior* or *Doctior, with more Piety or Learning*, at least he may depart *Jucundior*, with more pleasure
and lawful delight.

Lastly, to procure moderate profit to my self in com-
pensation of my pains. It was a proper question, which
plain dealing *Jacob* pertinently propounded to *Laban* his
Father in Law : *and now when shall I provide for mine*
10 *house also ?* Hitherto no Stationer hath lost by me, hereafter it will be high time for me (all things considered) to
Save for my self.

The matter following may be divided into *Real* and
Personal, though not according to the legal acception of the
words. By *Real*, I understand the commodities and observables of every County : by *Personal* the Characters of
those worthy men, who were Natives thereof. We begin
with a Catalogue of the particular heads whereof this book
doth consist, intending to shew, how they are *severally*
20 *useful*, and then I hope, if *good* as *single instruments*, they
will be the *better as tuned in a Consort*.

Alfred

ALFREDE the fourth Son to K. *Athelwolph* was born at
Wantage a market-town in this County. An excellent
scholar, though he was past *twelve years of age* before he
knew *one letter in the Book* ; and did not he *run fast* who
starting so *late* came *soon to the mark ?* He was a *Curious
Poet, excellent Musician*, a valiant and successeful Souldier,
who fought seven Battles against the *Danes* in one year,
and at last made them his Subjects by Conquest, and Gods
30 servants by Christianity. He gave the first *Institution*, or
(as others will have it) the best *Instauration* to the Univer-

sity of *Oxford*. A Prince who cannot be painted to the Life without his losse, no *words* reaching his *worth*.

He Divided
1. Every natural day (as to himself) into three parts, *eight hours* for his devotion, *eight hours* for his imployment, *eight hours* for his sleep and refection.
2. His *Revenues* into three parts, one for his expences in *War*, a second for the maintenance of his *Court*, and a third to be spended on *Pious uses*.   10
3. His *Land* into *Thirty two shires*, which number since is altered and increased.
4. His *Subjects* into *Hundreds*, and Tythings, consisting of *Ten persons*, mutually *Pledges* for their *Good behaviour* ; such being accounted suspitious for their *Life* and *Loyalty* that could not give such *Security*.

He left *Learning*, where he found *Ignorance* ; *Justice*, where he found *Oppression* ; *Peace*, where he found *Dis-* 20 *traction*. And having Reigned about Four and thirty years, He dyed and was buried at *Winchester*, *Anno* 901. He loved *Religion* more then *Superstition*, favoured *Learned men* more then *Lasie Monks*, which [perchance] was the cause that his *memory* is not loaden with *Miracles*, and He not solemnly Sainted with other *Saxon Kings* who far less deserved it.

(Bark-shire)

Cambridge

Cambridge is the chief credit of this County, as the University is of *Cambridge*. It is confess'd, that *Oxford* far 30 exceeds it for sweetness of situation ; and yet it may be maintained, that though there be *better* aire in *Oxford*, yet there is *more* in the Colledges of *Cambridge*. For, *Oxford* is an University in a Town, *Cambridge*, a Town in an University ; where the Colledges are not surrounded with the offensive embraces of Streets, but generally situated on the out-side, affording the better conveniency of private Walks and Gardens about them. But having formerly written of the fabricks of *Cambridge*, I forbear any further inlargement.

(Cambridge-shire)

Sir Hugh Calverley

SIR HUGH CALVELY born at *Calvely* in this County. Tradition makes him a man of *Teeth* and *Hands,* who would *Feed* as much as *two*, and *Fight* as much as *ten* men, his quick and strong *Appetite*, could *disgest* any thing but an *Injury*, so that killing a man, is reported the cause of his quitting this County, making hence for *London*, then for *France*. Here he became a most eminent Souldier, answering the Character our great Antiquary hath given him,

Arte militari ita in Galliâ inclaruit, ut vividæ ejus virtuti nihil fuit impervium.

I find *five* of his principall Atchievements.

1. When he was one of the *thirty English* in *France*, who in a duel encountred as many *Britans*.

2. When in the last of King *Edward* the third, being Governour of *Calice* he looked on, (his hands being tyed behind him by a Truce, yet in force for a Month,) and saw the *English* slain before his eyes, whose bloud he soon after revenged.

3. When in the first of King *Richard* the second, after an unfortunate voyage of our *English Nobility*, beaten home with a Tempest, he took *Bark bulloigne*

and *five* and *twenty* other *French-ships*, besides the
Castle of *Mark*, lately lost by negligence, which he
recovered.

4. When in the next year he spoiled *Estaples*, at a
   Fair-time, bringing thence so much Plunder as
   enriched the *Calicians* for many years after.

5. When he married the *Queen* of *Aragon*, which is
   most certain, her Armes being quartered on his
   Tomb, though I cannot satisfy the Reader in the
   Particularities thereof.

The certain date of his death is unknown, which by
proportion may be collected about the year 1388. After
which time, no mention of him, and it was as impossible
for such a spirit not to *be*, as not to be active.

(Ches-shire)

John Speed

JOHN SPEED was born at *Farrington* in this County as
his own Daughter hath informed me ; he was first bred
to a *handicraft*, and as I take it to a *Taylor*. I write not
this for *his* but *my own* disgrace, when I consider how far
his *Industry* hath outstript my *Ingenious Education*. Sir
Fulk Grevill, a great favourer of Learning, perceiving how
his *wide soul* was *stuffed* with too *narrow* an occupation,
first wrought his inlargement as the said Author doth
ingeniously confess,

> *Whose merits to me-ward I do acknowledge in setting this*
> *hand free from the daily imployments of a manuall*
> *Trade, and giving it his liberty thus to express the*
> *inclination of my mind, himself being the procurer of*
> *my present Estate.*

This is he who afterwards designed the *Maps* and com-

posed the *History of England*, though much help'd in both
(no shame to crave aid in a work too weighty for any ones
back to bear,) by Sir *Robert Cotton*, Master *Camden*, Master
Barkham and others. He also made the usefull *Genealogies*
preposed formerly to English Bibles in all Volumes, having
a Patent granted him from King *James*, in reward of his
great Labours, to receive the benefit thereof to him and his.
This was very beneficiall unto them by Composition with
the Company of Stationers, untill this Licentious age
10 neglecting all such Ingenious helps to understand Scripture,
and almost levelling (if not prevented) the propriety of all
Authors of Books. He dyed in *London Anno 1629* and
was buried in Saint *Giles* without *Criplegate*, in the same
Parish with Master *John Fox*, so that no *one* Church in
England, containeth the Corps of *two* such *usefull* and
voluminous Historians. Master *Josias Shute* Preach'd his
Funerall Sermon : and thus we take our leaves of *Father
Speed*, truly answering his name in both the acceptions
thereof for *Celerity* and *Success*.

20   (*Ches-shire*)

Sir·Richard Sutton

Sir Richard Sutton was born at *Presbury* in this
County, he is generally believed a *Knight*, though some
have suspected the same, but suppose him but *Esquire*.
He was one of a *Plentifull Estate* and *Bountifull Hand*.

It happened that *William Smith* Bishop of *Lincoln* began
Brasen-Nose-Colledge, but dyed before he had finished one
Nostrill thereof, leaving this *Sutton* his *Executor*, who over-
performed the *Bishops Will*, and compleated the *Foundation*
with his own liberall Additions thereunto. When the
30 following Verses were composed, in the *Person* of *Brasen-
Nose-Colledge*, the *Muses* seemed neither to *smile* nor

frown, but kept their *wonted countenance*. But take them
as they are.

> *Begun by one but finish'd by another,*
> Sutton *he was my* Nurse, *but* Smith *my* Mother :
> *Or if the Phrase more proper seem, say rather,*
> *That* Sutton *was my* Guardian, Smith *my* Father ;
> *'Cause equal Kindness they to me exprest,*
> *Better I neither love, love both the best.*
> *If* Both *they may be call'd, who had* one will,
> *What One design'd, the Other did fulfill.*
> *May such Testators live who Good intend,*
> *But if they dye, Heaven such* Exec'tors *send.*

10

This *Worthy Knight* being born in this *County*, deservedly
reflected upon his own *Country-men*, making them (and
those of *Lancashire*) most capable of Preferment. I collect
his death to have happened about the *middle* of the *Raign*
of King *Henry* the eighth.

(Ches-shire)

Thomas Jackson

THOMAS JACKSON, born of a good *Family* in this County
was designed to be a Merchant in *New-Castle*, till his
Parents were diverted by *Ralph* Lord *Eure*, and perswaded
to make him a Scholar. He was admitted first in *Queens
Colledge* in *Oxford*, and then became *Candidate* of a Fellowship in *Corpus Christi* ; knowing of the election but the
day before, he answered to admiration, and was chosen by
general consent.

20

Soon after, in all likelihood, he lost his life, being *drowned*
in the River, and taken out rather for desire of decent
burial, than with hope of any recovery : He was wrap'd
in the *Gowns* of his fellow *Students* (the best shrowd which
present love and need could provide him) and being
brought home to the Colledge, was revived by Gods blessing
on the care of Doctor *Chenil*, equally to all peoples joy and
admiration. His gratitude to the Fisher-men (who took

30

him up) extended to a revenue unto them during his life. Thus thankful to the Instrument, he was more to the Principal, striving to repay his life to that God who gave it him.

He was afterwards *Vicar* of *New Castle* (a *Factor for Heaven*, in the place where he was designed a *Merchant*) a Town full of men and opinions wherein he endeavoured to rectifie their Errors, and unite their Affections. At this distance was he chosen *President* of *Corpus Christi Colledge*, never knowing of the vacancy of the place, till by those Letters (which informed him) it was refilled with his election.

Here he lived piously, ruled peaceably, wrote profoundly, preached painfully. His Charity had no fault, if not of the largest size, oftentimes making the Receiver richer, than it left him that was the Donor thereof. Learn the rest of his praise from the Learned Writer of his Life, in whom nothing wanting, save the exact place of his birth, and date of his death, which hapned about the year, 1640.

(*Durham*)

Thomas Tusser

THOMAS TUSSER was born at *Riven-hall* in this County, of an ancient family (since extinct) if his own pen may be believed. Whilst as yet a Boy he lived in many Schools, *Wallingford*, Saint *Pauls*, *Eaton*, (whence he went to *Trinity hall* in *Cambridge*,) when a Man, in *Stafford-shire*, *Suffolk*, *Northfolk*, *Cambridge-shire*, *London*, and where not? so that this Stone of *Sisiphus* could gather no Moss. He was successively a *Musitian*, *School-master*, *Servingman*, *Husbandman*, *Grasier*, *Poet*, more skilfull in all, then thriving in any Vocation. He traded at large in *Oxen*, *Sheep*, *Dairies*, *Grain* of all kinds, to no profit. Whether he bought or sold, he lost, and when a *Renter impoverished* himself, and never *inriched* his Landlord. Yet hath he laid down excellent Rules in his *Book of Husbandry* and *Houswifery*, (so that the Observer thereof must be rich,) *in his own defence*. He *spread* his *Bread* with all sorts of *Butter*, yet none would *stick* thereon. Yet I hear no man to charge him with any vicious extravagancy, or visible carelessness, imputing his ill success to some occult cause in Gods counsel. Thus our English *Columella* might say with the Poet,

———— *Monitis sum minor ipse meis,*

None being better at the *Theory*, or worse at the *Practise* of Husbandry. I match him with *Thomas Church-yard*, they being *mark'd* alike in their *Poeticall parts*, living in the same time, and *statur'd* alike in their *Estates*, both *low enough* I assure you. I cannot find the certain date of his death, but collect it to be about 1580.

(*Essex*)

Francis Quarles

FRANCIS QUARLES Esquire, son to *James Quarles* Esquire, was born at *Stewards*, in the Parish of *Rumford* in this County, where his son (as I am inform'd) hath an Estate in expectancy. He was bred in *Cambridge*, and going over into *Ireland*, became Secretary to the Reverend *James Usher* Arch-bishop of *Armagh*. He was a most excellent Poet, and had a mind byassed to devotion. Had he been contemporary with *Plato*, (that great back-friend to Poets,) he would not onely have allowed him to live, but advanced him to an office in his *Common-wealth*.

Some Poets, if debarr'd profaness, wantonness, and Satyricalness, (that they may neither abuse God, themselves, nor their neighbours,) have their tongues cut out in

effect. Others onely trade in *wit at the second hand*, being all for translations, nothing for invention. Our *Quarles* was free from the faults of the first, as if he had drank of *Jordan* in stead of *Helicon*, and slept on mount *Olivet* for his *Pernassus*, and was happy in his own invention. His *visible Poetry* (I mean his *Emblems*) is excellent, catching therein the eye and fancy at one draught, so that he hath *out-Alciated* therein, in some mens judgement. His Verses on *Job* are done to the life, so that the Reader may see his
10 sores, and through them the anguish of his soul.

The troubles of *Ireland*, where his losses were great, forced his return hither, bearing his crosses with great patience; so that (according to the advice of Saint *Hierome*,) *Verba vertebat in opera*, and practiced the *Job* he had described, dying about the year 1643.

(Essex)

Hatfield House

Hatfield-house was first the Bishops of *Ely*, then the Kings, afterwards by exchange the Earls of *Salisbury*: For Situation, Building, Contrivance, Prospect, Air, and
20 all accommodations, inferiour to none in *England*. Within a little mile thereof lyeth a place called the *Vineyard*, where *nature* by the *Midwifery* of *Art*, is delivered of much pleasure; So that the *Reader* must be a *Seer*, before he can understand the perfection thereof. Had this place been in *Græcia*, or nigh *Rome*, where the luxuriant fancies of the Poets, being *subject-bound*, improve a *Tree* into a *Grove*, a *Grove* into a *Forrest*, a *Brook* into a *River*, and a *Pond* into a *Lake*; I say, had this *Vineyard* been there, it had disinherited *Tempe* of its honour, and hence the Poets
30 would have dated all their delights as from a Little Paradise, and Staple-place of earthly pleasure.

(Hartford-shire)

Richard Hackluit

RICHARD HACKLUIT, was born of an *ancient extract* in this County, whose Family hath flourished at . . . in good esteem. He was bred a *Student* in *Christ Church*, in *Oxford*, and after was *Prebendary* of *Westminster*, His *Genius* inclined him to the *Study of History*, and especially to the *Marine part* thereof, which made him keep constant Intelligence with the most noted *Seamen* of *Wapping*, until the day of his Death.

He set forth a large Collection of the English Sea Voyages, Ancient, Middle, Modern, taken partly out of private 10 *Letters*, which never were (or without his care had not been) printed. Partly out of Small *Treatises*, printed, and since irrecoverably lost, had not his providence preserved them. For some *Pamphlets* are produced, which for their *Cheapnesse* and *Smalnesse* men of the present neglect to buy, presuming they may procure them at their pleasure, which small Books, their *first* and *last* Edition being past, (like some Spirits that appear but once) cannot afterwards with any price or pains be recovered. In a word many of such useful Tracts of *Sea Adventures*, which before were scattered 20 as *several Ships*, Mr. *Hackluit* hath imbodied into a *Fleet*, divided into *three Squadrons*, so many several Volumes. A Work of great honour to *England*, it being possible that many *Ports* and *Islands* in *America* which being *base* and *barren*, bear only a bare name for the present, may prove rich places for the future. And then these Voyages will be produced and pleaded, as, good *Evidence* of their *belonging* to *England*, as first discovered and denominated by *English-men*. Mr. *Hackluit* dyed in the beginning of *King Iames* his *Reign*, leaving a fair estate to an unthrift *Son*, 30 who embezill'd it, on this token, that he vanted, that he cheated the covetous Usurer, *who had given him Spick and*

Span new money, for the Old Land of his Great Great Grand-father.

(*Hereford-shire*)

John Davies

JOHN DAVIES of *Hereford* (for so he constantly styled himself) was the greatest *Master* of the *Pen* that *England* in his age beheld, for

1. *Fast-writing*, so incredible his expedition.
2. *Fair-writing*, some minutes Consultation being required to decide, whether his Lines were written or printed.
3. *Close-writing*, A Mysterie indeed, and too Dark for my Dimme Eyes to discover.
4. *Various-writing*, *Secretary*, *Roman*, *Court*, and *Text*.

The *Poetical fiction* of *Briareus* the Gyant, who had an *hundred hands*, found a *Moral* in him, who could so cunningly and copiously disguise his aforesaid *Elemental hands*, that by mixing he could make them appear an *hundred*, and if not so many *sorts*, so many *Degrees of Writing*. Yet had he lived longer he would modestly have acknowledged Mr. *Githings* (who was his Schollar and also born in this County) to excel him in that faculty, whilst the other would own, no such odious *Eminencie*, but rather gratefully return the credit to his *Master* again. Sure I am, when two such *Transcendent Pen-masters* shall again come to be born in the *same shire*, they may even serve *fairly* to *engross* the *will* and *testament* of the *expiring Universe*. Our *Davies* had also some pretty excursions into *Poetry* and could *flourish matter* as well as *Letters*, with his *Fancy* as well as with his *Pen*. He dyed at *London* in the midst of the *Reign* of King *James*, and lyeth buryed in St. *Giles* in the *fields*.

(*Hereford-shire*)

Sir Robert Cotton

SIR ROBERT COTTON Knight and Baronet son to *Iohn Cotton* Esquire was born at *Cunnington* in this County discended by the *Bruces* from the bloud Royall *of Scotland*. He was bred in *Trinity Colledge in Cambridge* where when a youth ; He discovered his inclination to the studie of *Antiquity* (they must *Spring early* who would *sprout* high in that *knowledge*) and afterwards attained to such eminency, that sure I am he had no *Superiour* if any his *equal* in the skill thereof.

But that which rendred him deservedly to the praise of present and future times, yea the wonder of our own and forreign Nations, was his collection of his Library in *Westminster*, equally famous for

1. *Rarity*, having so many Manuscript *Originals*, or else *copies* so exactly Transcribed, that, *Reader*, I must confesse he must have more skill then I have to distinguish them.
2. *Variety*, He that beholdeth their *number*, would admire they should be *rare*, and he that considereth their *rarity* will more admire at their *number*.
3. *Method*, Some Libraries are *labyrinths*, not for the *multitude*, but *confusion* of Volumes, where a stranger *seeking* for a book may quickly loose himself, whereas these are so exactly methodized (under the heads of the twelve *Roman* Emperours) that it is harder for one to misse then to hit any Author he desireth.

But what addeth a luster to all the rest is the favourable accesse thereunto, for such as bring any competency of *skill* with them, and leave *thankfulness* behind them. Some *Antiquaries* are so jealous of their books, as if every hand which *toucheth* would *ravish* them, whereas here no such suspition of *ingenious persons*. And here give me leave to register my self amongst the meanest of those who through the favour of Sir *Thomas Cotton* (inheriting as well the *courtesie* as *estate* of his Father Sir *Robert*) have had admittance into that *worthy treasury*.

Yea, most true it is what one saith, That the grandest Antiquaries have here fetcht their *materials*.

—————— *Omnis ab illo*
Et Camdene *tua, &* Seldeni *gloria crevit,*
Camden to him, to him doth *Selden* owe,
Their Glory, what they got from him did grow.

I have heard that there was a design driven on in the *Popes Conclave* after the death of Sir *Robert*, to compasse this *Library* to be added to that in *Rome*, which if so, what a *Vatican* had there been within the *Vatican*, by the accession thereof. But blessed be God the Project did miscarry to the honour of our Nation, and advantage of the Protestant Religion.

For therein are contained many *privaties* of *Princes*, and *transactions* of State, insomuch that I have been informed, that the *Fountains* have been *fain* to fetch *water* from the *stream*; and the Secretaries of State, and Clerks of the Council, glad from hence to borrow back again many *Originals*, which being lost by casualty or negligence of Officers, have here been recovered and preserved. He was a man of a publick spirit, it being his principal endevour in all Parliaments (wherein he served so often) That the *prerogative* and *priviledge* might run in their due channel, and in truth he did cleave the pin betwixt the *Soveraign* and the *Subject*. He was wont to say, *That he himself had the least share in himself*, whilest his *Country* and *Friends* had the greatest interest in him. He died at his house in *Westminster, May* the 6. *Anno Domini, 1631*. in the *61* year of his Age, though one may truely say, *his age was adequate to the continuance of the Creation*, such was his exact skill in all antiquity. By *Elizabeth* daughter and co-heire of *William Brocas* Esquire, he had onely one son, Sir *Thomas* now living, who by *Margaret* daughter to the Lord *William Howard* (Grandchild to *Thomas* Duke of *Norfolke*) hath one son *Iohn Cotton* Esquire, and two daughters *Lucie* and *Francis*. The *Opera posthuma* of this worthy Knight, are lately set forth in one Volume to the great profit of posterity.

(Huntington-shire) 10

Sir Philip Sidney

SIR PHILIP SIDNEY. Reader, I am resolved not to part him from his Father, such the Sympathy betwixt them, living and dying both within the compass of the same year. Otherwise, this Knight in relation to my Book, may be termed an *Ubiquitary*, and appear amongst *Statesmen*, *Souldiers*, *Lawyers*, *Writers*, yea *Princes* themselves, being (though not elected) in election to be King of *Poland*, which place he declined, preferring rather to be a Subject to Queen *Elizabeth*, than a *Soveraign* beyond the Seas.

He was born at *Pensherst* in this County, son to Sir 20 *Henry Sidney* (of whom before) and Sisters Son to *Robert* Earl of *Leicester*, bred in *Christs Church* in *Oxford*. Such his appetite to Learning, that he could never be fed fast enough therewith ; and so quick and strong his digestion, that he soon turned it into wholsome nourishment, and thrived healthfully thereon.

His homebred abilities travel perfected with forraign accomplishments, and a sweet Nature set a glosse upon both. He was so essential to the English Court, that it seemed maimed without his company, being a compleat 30 Master of Matter and Language, as his *Arcadia* doth evidence.

I confesse I have heard some of modern pretended Wits cavil thereat, meerly because they made it not themselves : such who say, that his Book, is the *occasion* that many *pretious hours* are otherwise spent no *better*, must acknowledge it also the cause, that many *idle hours* are otherwise spent no *worse*, than in reading thereof.

At last, leaving the Court, he followed the Camp, being made Governor of *Flushing*, under his Uncle Earl of *Leicester*. But the Walls of that City (though high and strong) could not confine the activity of his mind, which must into the Field, and before *Zutphen* was unfortunately slain with a shot, in a *small skirmish*, which we may sadly tearm a *great battel*, considering our heavy losse therein. His Corps being brought over into *England*, was buried in the Quire of St. *Pauls* with general lamentation.

(*Kent*)

William Harvey

WILLIAM HARVEY, Son of *Thomas Harvey*, was born at *Folkston* in this County. His Father had a *Week* of Sons ; whereof this *William* bred to learning, was the eldest ; his other brethren being bound Apprentices in *London*, and all at last ended in effect in Merchants. They got great Estates, and made their Father the Treasurer thereof, who being as skilful to purchase Land, as they to gain Money, kept, employed, and improved their gainings to their great advantage ; so that he survived to see the meanest of them, of far greater estate than himself.

Our *William* was bred in *Caius* Colledge in *Cambridge*, where he proceeded Doctor of Physick. Five years also he studied at *Padua*, making a good Composition of *Forraign* and *Domestick* learning : So that afterwards he was (for many years) Physician to King *Charles* the First. And not only *Doctor Medecinæ*, but *Doctor Medicorum*.

For this was he that first found out the *Circulation of the Blood* ; an opinion which entred into the World with great disadvantages. For first, none will be acquainted with strangers at the first sight, as persons generally suspected ; as if to be *unknown*, were part of being *guilty*. Secondly, the Grandees of this Profession were of the opposite judgement, heavy enough without any *Argument* to *overlay* (and so to *stifle*) any Infant opinion by their Authority.

But, *Truth*, though it may be questioned for a *Vagrant*, carrieth a Passport along with it for its own vindication. Such have since shaken friendly hands with *Doctor Harvey*, which at first tilted *Pens* against him. And amongst the rest *Riolanus* that learned Physician, if not *Ambabus ulnis*, with *one Arm* at the least doth embrace his opinion, and partly consent thereunto.

This Doctor, though living a Batchelor, may be said to have left three hopeful Sons to posterity ; his Books,

1. *De circulatione sanguinis*, which I may call his *Son* and *Heir* ; the Doctor living to see it at full age, and generally received.
2. *De generatione*, as yet in its minority ; but, I assure you growing up apace into publick credit.
3. *De Ovo*, as yet in the nonage thereof, but infants may be men in due time.

It must not be forgotten, that this Doctor had made a good progresse, to lay down a Practice of Physick, conformable to his *Thesis*, of the *Circulation of Blood* ; but was plundered of his Papers in our Civil War : Unhappy dissentions, which not onely murdered many then alive ; but may be said by this, (call it *mischief* or *mischance*) to have destroyed more not yet born, whose Diseases might have been either prevented or removed, if his worthy pains had come forth into the Publick : And I charitably presume, that grateful posterity will acknowledge the improvements of this opinion, as Superstructures on his Foundation ; and thankfully pay the fruit to his memory, who *watered*, *planted*, (not to say *made*) the *root* of this discovery.

(Kent)

John Bradford

JOHN BRADFORD was born at *Manchester*, in this County, and bred first a Lawyer in the Inns of Court, and for a time did solicite Suits for Sr. *John Harrington*: afterwards, saith my *Authour*, *ex Rixoso Causidico mitissimus Christi Apostolus*: going to *Cambridg* a man in maturity, and ability, the University by special Grace bestowed on him the Degree of Master of *Art*: and so may he be said to Commence, not only *per saltum*, but *per volatum*. The Jesuit doth causlesly urge this his *short standing* for an Argument of his *little understanding*; whereas he had alwayes been a hard Student from his youth : and his Writings and his Disputings give a sufficient Testimony of his Learning.

It is a demonstration to me, that he was of a sweet temper, Because *Persons* who will hardly afford a good Word to a Protestant, saith, *that he seemed to be of a more soft and milde nature than many of his fellowes*. Indeed he was a most holy and mortified man, who secretly in his closet would so weep for his sinnes, one would have thought he would never have smiled again : and then appearing, in publick, he would be so harmlesly pleasant, one would think he had never wept before : But Mr. *Fox* his pains have given the pens of all Posterity a *Writ of ease*, to meddle no more with this Martyr, who suffered *Anno Dom.* 1555.

(Lancashire)

Lawrence Chaderton

LAWRENCE CHADERTON was born at *Chaderton* in this County, of ancient, and wealthy Parentage, but much nuzled up in Popish Superstition. He was intended for a Lawyer, and in order thereunto, brought up some time in the *Inns of Court*, till he changed his profession, and admitted himself in *Christs Colledge* in *Cambridge*. His Father hearing that he had altered his place, studies, and Religion, sent him a Poke with a groat therein, for him to go a begging therewith, disinheriting him of that fair estate, which otherwise had descended upon him. But God who 10 taketh men up *when their Fathers and Mothers forsake them*, provided him a comfortable subsistance, when chosen Fellow of the *Colledge*. He was for many years Lecturer at St. *Clements* in *Cambridge*, with great profit to his Auditors, afterwards made by the Founder first Master of *Emanuel*. He was chosen by the *Non-Conformists* to be one of their *four Representatives* in *Hampton-court* conference, and was afterwards employed one of the Translators of the Bible. He had a *plain* but *effectual* way of Preaching. It happened that he visiting his friends, preached in this 20 his *Native Countrey*, where the Word of God (as in the dayes of *Samuell*) was very pretious. And concluded his Sermon which was of two hours continuance at least, with words to this effect. *That he would no longer trespasse upon their Patience.* Whereupon all the Auditory cryed out, (wonder not if hungry people craved more meat) *for God Sake Sir Go on, go on.* Hereat Mr. *Chaderton* was surprised into a longer Discourse, beyond his expectation, in Satisfaction of their importunity, and (though on a sudden) performed it to their *contentment* and his *commendation*. 30 Thus, *constant Preachers*, like *good house-keepers*, can never be taken so unprovided, but that, (though they make not

a *plentiful Feast*) they can give *wholsome food* at a short
warning.

He commenced Dr. in Divinity, when *Frederick* Prince
Palatine (who married the Lady *Elizabeth*) came to *Cam-
bridge*. What is said of *Mount Caucasus*, that it was never
seen without Snowe on the Top, was true of this *Reverend
Father*, whom none of our Fathers generation knew in the
Universitie, before he was gray headed, yet he never used
Spectacles till the day of his death, being Ninety four years
10 of age.

He was not disheartned with that common saying, *he
that resigneth his place before his death, buryeth himself alive*,
but put off his Clothes long before he went to bed, divested
himself of the Master-ship of *Emanuel Colledge*, that so he
might see a worthy successor in his life time. The blessing
which befell *Job*, was in some sort appliable unto him, he
saw his Successors to the *fourth generation*. I mean Doctor
Presson, and after his Death Doctor *Sancroft*, and after his
death Doctor *Holesworth*, who preached his Funeral Sermon
20 *Anno* 1640. about the Ninety fourth year of his age.

(Lancashire)

George Villiers

GEORGE VILLIERS was born at *Brooksby* in this County,
fourth son to his father Sir *George Villiers* and second son to
his Mother *Mary Beaumont*. Being debarred (by his late
Nativity) from his fathers lands, he was happy in his
Mothers love, maintaining him in *France*, till he returned
one of the compleatest Courtiers in Christendom, his body
and behaviour mutually gracing one another.

Sir *Tho. Lake* may be said to have ushered him to the
30 *English* Court, whilest the Lady *Lucy* Countess of *Bedford*
led him by the one hand, and *William* Earl of *Pembroke*

by the other, supplying him with a support far above his patrimonial income. The truth is, *Sommersets* growing daily more wearisome, made *Villiers* hourly more welcome to K. *James*.

Soon after he was knighted, created successively *Baron Viscount Villiers*, Earl, Marquess, Duke of *Buckingham*, and to bind all his *honours* the better together, the noble *Garter* was bestowed upon him. And now *Offices* at *Court*, (not being already *void*) were *voided* for him. The *Earl of Worcester* was perswaded to part with his *place* of *Master* 10 of the *horse*, as the *Earl of Nottingham* with his *Office* of *Admiral*, and both conferred on the Duke.

He had a numerous and beautiful female kindred, so that there was hardly a noble Stock in *England* into which one of these his *Cients* was not grafted. Most of his *Neices* were matched with little more portion then their *Uncles* smiles, the forerunner of some good *Office* or *Honour* to follow on their *Husbands*. Thus with the same act did he both gratifie his kindred, and fortifie himself with noble alliance. 20

It is seldome seen that two Kings, (father and Son) tread successively in the same *Tract* as to a *Favourite* ; but here King *Charles*, had as high a kindness for the *Duke* as K. *James*. Thenceforward he became the *Plenipotentiary* in the *English Court*, some of the *Scottish* Nobility making room for him, by their seasonable departure out of this Life. The Earl of *Bristoll* was justled out, the *Bishop* of *Lincoln* cast flat on the Floor, the Earls of *Pembroke* and *Carlisle* content to shine beneath him, *Holland* behind him, none even with, much lesse before him. 30

But it is generally given to him, who is the *little God at the Court*, to be the *great Devil in the Countrey*. The Commonalty hated him with a perfect hatred, and all miscarriages in *Church* and *State*, at Home, Abroad, at Sea and Land were charged on his want of Wisdom, Valour or Loyalty.

John Felton a melancholy malecontented Gentleman, and a sullen Souldier, apprehending himself injured, could find no other way to revenge his conceived wrongs, then by writing them with a point of a Knife in the heart of the Duke, whom he stabbed at *Portsmouth. Anno Dom.* 1620. It is hard to say how many of this Nation were guilty of this murther, either by publick praising or private ap-
10 proving thereof.

His person from head to foot could not be charged with any blemish, save that some *Hypercriticks* conceived his Brows somewhat over pendulous, a cloud which in the judgement of others was by the beams of his Eyes sufficiently dispelled. The Reader is remitted for the rest of his Character, to the exquisite Epitaph on his magnificent Monument, in the Chappel of *Henry* the Seventh.

(*Leicester-shire*)

Jervasius Scroop

JERVASIUS SCROOP *Miles*.]
20   He ingaged with his Majesty in *Edge-hill-fight*, where he received *twenty six* wounds, and was left on the ground amongst the dead. Next day his Son *Adrian* obtained leave from the King to find and fetch off his Fathers Corps and his hopes pretended no higher then to a decent Interment thereof.

Hearty seeking makes happy finding. Indeed, some more commended the affection, than the judgement of the Young Gentleman, conceiving such a search in vain, amongst many naked bodies, with wounds disguised from
30 themselves, and where pale Death had confounded all complexions together.

However he having some general hint of the place where

his Father fell, did light upon his body, which had some
heat left therein. This heat was with rubbing, within few
Minutes, improved into motion ; that motion within some
hours into sense ; that sense, within a day into speech ;
that speech within certain Weeks, into a perfect recovery,
living more then *ten* years after, a Monument of Gods
mercy and his Sons affection.

He always after carried his Arme in a Scarfe, and loss
of blood made him look very pale, as a Messenger come
from the Grave, to advise the Living to prepare for Death. 10
The effect of his Story, I received from his own mouth, in
Lincolne-colledge.

(Lincolne-shire)

Old St. Paul's

THIS is the only *Cathedral* in *Christendome* Dedicated
solely to that Saint : Great the Pillars (little Legs would
bowe under so big a body) and small the Windows thereof,
Darknesse in those dayes being conceived to raise Devotion,
besides it made artificial Lights to appear with the more
Solemnity. It may be called the *Mother Church* indeed,
having one Babe in her Body St. *Faiths*, and another in her 20
Arms St. *Gregories*. Surely such, who repair to Divine
Service in St. *Faiths*, may there be well minded of their
Mortality, being living *People*, surrounded with the *Anti-
peristatis* of the Dead both above and beneath them. For
the present I behold St. *Pauls* Church, as one struck with
the Dead Palsie on one side, the East part and Quire thereof
being quick and alive, well maintained and repaired, whilst
the West part is ruinous and ready to fall down. Little
hopes it will be repaired in its old Decayes, which is decayed
in its new Reparations, and being formerly an Ornament, 30
is now an Eyesore to the City ; not to say unto the Citizens

in general, some being offended that it is in so *bad*, and others
that it is in no *worse* Condition.

The Repairing of this Church was a worthy Monument
of the Piety and Charity of Arch-Bishop *Laud*, not only
procuring the Bounty of others, but expending his own
Estate thereon. We dispair not but that his Majesties
Zeal in commending this work to their care, will in due
time meet with the Forward Bounty of the Citizens. It is
no sin to wish, that those who have plundered the *Cloak*
10 and *Cover* of St. *Pauls* (not left behind *by*, but) violently
taken *from* him, might be compelled to make him a new
one of their own Cost, at leastwise to contribute more then
ordinary proportions thereunto.

(London)

London Bridge

THE Middle thereof is properly in *none*, the *two* ends in
two Counties *Middlesex* and *Surrey*. Such who only see it
beneath where it is a *Bridge*, cannot suspect it should be a
Street, and such who behold it *above* where it is a *Street*,
cannot beleive it is a *Bridge*. It was made with great cost,
20 and is maintained with daily charge against the Batery
and Assault of the Tide : The sad Riddle is generally
known to all, which happened here some *twenty* years since,
when a lamentable fire could not be quenched, because
there was such store of Water, hindering all accesse thereunto.

(London)

Sir Thomas More

SIR THOMAS MORE was, *Anno Domini* 1480 born in
Milkstreet London, (the *brightest Star* that ever shined in
that *Via lactea*) sole Son to Sir *John More* Knight, one of
30 the Justices of the *Kings Bench*.

Some have reported him of mean parentage, meerly

from a mistake of a modest word, in an Epitaph of his own making on his Monument in *Chelsey* Church.

Where *Nobilis* is taken not in the *civil* but *Common Law* sense, which alloweth none Noble under the degree of Barons. Thus men cannot be too wary what they inscribe on Tombs, which may prove a Record (though not in *Law*, in *History*) to posterity.

He was bred first in the Family of Arch-bishop *Morton*, then in *Canterbury Colledge* (now taken into *Christ Church*) in *Oxford*, where he profited more in *two*, then many in *ten* years continuance.

Thence he removed to an Inn of Chancery called *New Inn*, and from thence to *Lincolns Inn*, where he became a *double Reader*. Then did his worth prefer him to be Judge in the *Sheriffe of Londons* Court, whilst a Pleader in others. And although he only chose such causes which appeared just to his Conscience, and never took Fee of Widow, Orphane or poor person ; he gained in those days *four hundred* pounds *per annum*.

Being made a Member of the House of Commons, he opposed King *Henry* the Seventh, about money for the Marriage of his Daughter *Margaret* : Whereat the King was much discontented, when a Courtier told him, *that a beardlesse Boy* (*beard* was never the true Standard of *brains*) *had obstructed his desires*. Which King being as certain, but more secret then *his son* in his revenge, made *More* the mark of his Displeasure, who to decline his anger had travelled beyond the seas, had not the Kings going into another World stopped his journey.

King *Henry* the Eighth coming to the Crown, and desirous to ingratiate himself by preferring popular and deserving persons, Knighted Sir *Thomas*, and made him Chancelour of the Dutchy of *Lancaster*, the Kings personal patrimony.

Finding him *faithfull in lesser matters* (according to the method of the Gospel) he made him in effect Ruler of all. when Lord Chancelour of *England* ; a place wherein he demeaned himself with great integrity, and with no less expedition. In testimony of the later, it is recorded, that calling for the next cause, it was returned unto him, there are no more to be heard, all Suits in that Court depending, and ready for hearing, being finally determined. Whereon a Rhythmer,

10
> *When* More *some years had Chancelor been,*
> *No more suits did remain,*
> *The same shall never more be seen,*
> *Till* More *be there again.*

Falling into the Kings displeasure for not complying with him about the Queens divorce, he seasonably resigned his Chancellours Place, and retired to his House in *Chelsey*, chiefly imploying himself in writing against those who were reputed Hereticks. And yet it is observed to his Credit (by his great friend *Erasmus*) that whilest he was Lord
20 Chancellor no *Protestant* was put to death, and it appears by some passages in his *Utopia*, that it was against his mind that any should lose their Lives for their Consciences.

He rather soyled his Fingers then dirtied his hands in the matter of the holy Maid of *Kent*, and well wiped it off again. But his *refusing* (*or rather not accepting*) the Oath of Supremacy, stuck by him, for which he was 16. Months imprisoned in the *Tower*, bearing his afflictions with remarkable patience. He was wont to say that his *natural temper was so tender, that he could not indure a philip* ; But
30 a supernatural *Principle* (we see) can countermand, yea help natural imperfections.

In his time (as till our Memory) *Tower* Prisoners were not dyeted on their own, but on the Kings charges ; The Lieutenant of the *Tower* providing their Fare for them.

And when the Lieutenant said that he was sorry that Commons were no better, *I like* (said Sir *Thomas*) *Your Dyet very well,* and if I dislike it, *I pray turn me out of Dores.*

Not long after he was beheaded on *Tower hill,* 153.. He left not above *one hundred* pounds a year Estate, perfectly hating Covetousnesse as may appear by his refusing of *four* or *five thousand pounds* offered him by the Clergy. Among his Latin Books his *Utopia* beareth the Bell, containing the *Idea* of a compleat Common-wealth in an Imaginary Island (but pretended to be lately discovered in *America*) and that so lively counterfeited, that many at the reading thereof mistook it for a real truth. Insomuch, that many great Learned men, as *Budeus,* and *Johannes Paludanus,* upon a fervent zeal, wished that some excellent *Divines* might be sent thither to preach *Christs* Gospel ; yea, there were here amongst us at home sundry good men and Learned *Divines,* very desirous to undertake the Voyage to bring the People to the Faith of Christ, whose manners they did so well like.

By his only Son Mr. *John More,* he had *five* Grandchildren, *Thomas* and *Augustin* born in his Life time, who proved zealous Romanists ; *Edward Thomas* and *Bartholomew* (born after his Death) were firm Protestants, and *Thomas* a married Minister of the Church of *England.*

(*London*)

Edmund Spenser

EDMOND SPENCER born in this City, was brought up in *Pembroke-hall* in *Cambridge,* where he became an excellent Scholar, but especially most happy in English Poetry, as his works do declare. In which the many *Chaucerisms* used (for I will not say affected by him) are thought by the ignorant to be *blemishes*, known by the learned to be *beauties* to his book ; which notwithstanding had been more salable, if more conformed to our modern language.

There passeth a story commonly told and believed, that *Spencer* presenting his Poems to Queen *Elizabeth* : She highly affected therewith, commanded the Lord *Cecil* Her Treasurer, to give him an *hundred* pound ; and when the Treasurer (a good Steward of the Queens money) alledged that sum was too much, then give *him* (quoth the Queen) *what is reason* ; to which the Lord consented, but was so busied, belike, about matters of higher concernment, that *Spencer* received no reward ; Whereupon he presented this petition in a small piece of paper to the Queen in her Progress,

> *I was promis'd on a time,*
> *To have reason for my rhyme ;*
> *From that time unto this season,*
> *I receiv'd nor rhyme nor reason.*

Hereupon the Queen gave strict order (not without some check to her Treasurer) for the present payment of the hundred pounds, she first intended unto him.

He afterwards went over into *Ireland*, Secretary to the Lord *Gray*, Lord Deputy thereof ; and though that his office under his Lord was lucrative, yet got he no estate, but saith my Author, *Peculiari Poetis fato semper cum paupertate conflictatus est.* So that it fared little better with him, then with *William Xilander* the *German*, (a most excellent Linguist, Antiquary, Philosopher and Mathematician,) who was so poor, that (as *Thuanus* saith) he was thought, *fami non famæ scribere.*

Returning into *England*, he was robb'd by the Rebels of that little he had, and dying for grief in great want, *Anno* 1598. was honorably buried nigh *Chaucer* in *Westminster*, where this Distick concludeth his Epitaph on his monument,

Anglica te vivo vixit plausit-
    que poesis,
Nunc moritura timet te
    moriente mori.
	Whilst thou didst live, liv'd
	    English poetry,
	Which fears, now thou art
	    dead, that she shall die.

Nor must we forget, that the expence of his funeral and monument, was defrayed at the sole charge of *Robert*, first of that name, Earl of *Essex*.

(*London*) 10

Edward Allin

EDWARD ALLIN was born in the aforesaid Parish near *Devonshire-house*, where now is the sign of the *Pie*. He was bred a Stage-player, a Calling which many have condemned, more have questioned, some few have excused, and far fewer consciencious people have commended. He was the *Roscius* of our age, so acting to the life, that he made any part (especially a Majestick one) to become him. He got a very great Estate, and in his old age following Christs Councel, (on what forcible motive belongs not to me to enquire) *He made friends of his unrighteous Mammon.* 20 Building therewith a fair Colledge at *Dulwich* in *Kent*, for the relief of poor people.

Some I confess count it built on a *foundred* foundation, seeing in a spiritual sense none is good and lawfull money save what is honestly and industrously gotten ; but perchance such who condemn Master *Allin* herein, have as bad Shillings in the bottome of their own bags if search were made therein ; sure I am, no Hospital is tyed with better or stricter laws, that it may not *Sagg* from the intention of the Founder. The poor of his native Parish 30 Saint *Buttolph Bishopgate* have a priviledge to be provided for therein before others. Thus he who out-acted others

in his life, out-did himself before his death, which happened
Anno Domini [26].

(London)

Edward I

EDWARD the first was born in *Westminster*, being a
Prince placed by the posture of his nativity, betwixt a *weak
Father*, and a *wilful Son*. Yet he needed no such advantage
for foils to set forth his real worth. He was surnamed
Longshanks, his *step* being another mans *stride*, and was
very high in stature. And though oftimes such who are
built *four stories high* are observed to have little in their
cock-loft, yet was he a most judicious man in all his undertakings, equally wise to plot, as valiant to perform, and
(which under Divine Providence was the result of both,)
happy in success at *Sea*, at *Land*, at *Home*, *Abroad*, in
War, in *Peace*. He was so fortunate with his *Sword* at
the beginning of his raign, that he awed all his enemies
with his *Scabbard*, before the end thereof. In a word he
was a Prince of so much merit that nothing under a *Chronicle*
can make his compleat *Character*.

(Westminster)

Benjamin Jonson

BENIAMIN JOHNSON was born in this City. Though I
cannot with all my industrious inquiry *find him* in his
cradle, I can *fetch him* from his *long coats*. When a *little
child* he lived in *Harts-horn-lane* near *Charing-cross*, where
his Mother married a *Bricklayer* for her Second husband.

He was first bred in a private school in Saint *Martins*
Church, then in *Westminster school*, witness his own
Epigram ;

> Camden, *most reverend Head, to whom I owe*
> *All that I am in Arts, all that I know.*
> *How nothing's that, to whom my Country owes*
> *The great renown and* Name *wherewith she goes*, &c.

He was *Statutably* admitted into Saint *Johns-colledge* in *Cambridge*, (as many years after incorporated a honorary Member of *Christ-church* in *Oxford*) where he continued but *few weeks* for want of further maintenance, being fain to return to the trade of his father in law. And let not them blush that have, but those that have not a lawful calling. He help'd in the building of the new structure of *Lincolns-Inn*, when having a *Trowell* in his hand, he had a *book* in his pocket.

Some gentlemen pitying that his parts should be buried under the rubbish of so mean a Calling, did by their bounty manumise him freely to follow his own ingenuous inclinations. Indeed his parts were not so *ready* to *run of themselves* as *able* to *answer the spur*, so that it may be truly said of him, that he had an *Elaborate wit* wrought out by his own industry. He would sit silent in learned company, and suck in (besides *wine*) their several humors into his observation. What was *ore* in others, he was able to refine to himself.

He was paramount in the Dramatique part of Poetry, and taught the *Stage* an exact conformity to the laws of Comedians. His Comedies were above the *Volge*, (which are onely tickled with down right obscenity) and took not so well at the *first stroke* as at the *rebound*, when beheld the second time ; yea they will endure reading, and that with due commendation, so long as either *ingenuity* or *learning* are fashionable in our *Nation*. If his *later* be not so spriteful and vigorous as his *first pieces*, all that are old will, and all that desire to be old, should excuse him therein.

He was not very happy in his children, and most happy in those which died first, though none lived to survive him. This he bestowed as part of an Epitaph on his eldest son, dying in infancy.

> *Rest in soft peace and Ask'd, say here doth lye,*
> Ben Johnson *his best piece of* Poetry.

He dyed *Anno Domini* 1638. And was buried about the
Belfry in the *Abby-church* at *Westminster*.

(Westminster)

John Fastolfe

JOHN FASTOLFE Knight, was a native of this County, as
I have just cause to believe, though some have made him
a *French-man*, meerly, because he was Baron of *Sineginle*
in *France*, on which account they may rob *England* of
many other *Worthies*. He was a *Ward* (and that the last)
to *John* Duke of *Bedford*, a sufficient evidence to such who
understand *time* and *place* to prove him of *English extraction*.
To avouch him by many arguments valiant, is to maintain
that the sun is bright, though since the *Stage* hath been
over bold with his memory, making him a *Thrasonical Puff*,
and emblem of *Mock-valour*.

True it is Sir *John Oldcastle* did first bear the brunt of
the one, being made the *make-sport* in all plays for a *coward*.
It is easily known out of what *purse* this black *peny* came.
The *Papists* railing on him for a *Heretick*, and therefore he
must also be a *coward*, though indeed he was a *man* of *arms*,
every inch of him, and as valiant as any in his age.

Now as I am glad that Sir *John Oldcastle* is *put out*, so
I am sorry that Sir *John Fastolfe* is *put in*, to relieve his
memory in this base service, to be the *anvil* for every *dull
wit* to strike upon. Nor is our Comedian excusable, by
some alteration of his name, writing him Sir *John Falstafe*,
(and making him the *property* of *pleasure* for King *Henry*
the fifth, to abuse) seeing the *vicinity* of sounds intrench
on the memory of *that worthy Knight*, and few do heed the
inconsiderable difference in spelling of their name. He was
made *Knight of the Garter* by King *Henry* the sixth, and
died about the second year of his reign.

(Norfolk)

John Baconthorpe

JOHN BACONTHORPE was born in a *Village* so called in
this County, bred a *Carmelite* in the *Convent* of *Blackney*,
and afterwards studied first in *Oxford*, then in *Paris*, one
remarkable on many accounts. First for the *Dwarfishness*
of his stature,

Scalpellum calami atramentum charta libellus,

His *Pen-knife*, *Pen*, *Ink-horn*, one sheet of *Paper*, and any
of his *books* would amount to his full height. As for all the
books of his own making, put together, their *burden* were
more then his *body* could bear.   10

Secondly, for his *high spirit* in his *low body*. Indeed his
soul had but a small *Diocess* to *visit*, and therefore might
the better attend the effectual informing thereof. I have
heard it delivered by a learned *Doctor in Physick*, (at the
Anatomy lecture in *London*) who a little before had been
present at the Emboweling and Embalming of Duke
Hamilton and the Lord *Capel*, that the heart of the former
was the largest, the latter the least he had ever beheld,
inferring hence, that contracted spirits act with the greatest
vigorousness.   20

Thirdly, for his *high title*, wherewith he was generally
termed the *resolute Doctor*. *Two* sorts of people he equally
disliked, *Scepticks* who are of *none* ; and *unconstant people*
who are [successively] of *all opinions*, and whilst others
turned about like the *Wheel*, he was as fixed as the *Axletree*
in his own judgement. Yet this his *resoluteness* was not
attended with censuring of such who were of another
Opinion, where equal probability on either side allowed
a latitude to dissent.

He groaped after *more light then he saw*, saw more than 30
he durst speak of, spake of more then he was thanked for
by those of his superstitious Order, amongst whom (saith

Bale) neither before, nor after, arose the like for *learning* and *religion*. Most agree in the *time* of his *death, Anno* 1346. though dissenting in the *place* of his *burial*, assigning *Blackney, Norwich, London,* the several places of his Interment.

(Norfolk)

John Fletcher

JOHN FLETCHER Son of *Richard Fletcher* D.D. was (as by proportion of time is collectible) born in this County, before his Father was Bishop of *Bristol* or *London,* and
10 whilst as yet he was Dean of *Peterborough.* He had an excellent wit, which the back-friends to Stage-plays will say, was *neither idle, nor well imploy'd.* For he and *Francis Beaumont* Esquire, like *Castor* and *Pollux,* (most happy when in conjunction) raised the *English,* to equal the *Athenian* and *Roman* Theater ; *Beaumont* bringing the *ballast* of judgement, *Fletcher* the *sail* of phantasie, both compounding a Poet to admiration.

Meeting once in a Tavern, to contrive the rude draught of a Tragedy, *Fletcher* undertook *to kill the King* therein,
20 whose words being over-heard by a listener (though his Loyalty not to be blamed herein) he was accused of High Treason, till the mistake soon appearing, that the plot was onely against a Drammatick and Scenical King, all wound off in merriment.

Nor could it be laid to *Fletcher's* charge, what *Ajax* doth to *Ulysses.*

Nihil hic Diomede *remoto.*   *When* Diomede *was gone,*
                                  He could do nought alone.

For surviving his partner, he wrote good Comedies him-
30 self, though inferiour to the former ; and no wonder, if a single thread was not so strong as a twisted one. He died

(as I am inform'd) in *London* of the plague in the first of
King *Charles*, 1625.

(Northampton-shire)

Oxford

THE Colleges in *Oxford*, advantaged by the vicinity of
fair *Free-stone*, do for the generality of their structure
carry away the credit from all in Christendom, and equal
any for the largness of their endowments.

It is not the least part of *Oxfords* happiness, that a moity
of her Founders were Prelates, (whereas *Cambridge* hath
but three Episcopal Foundations, *Peter-house, Trinity-hall*, 10
and *Jesus*) who had an experimental knowledge, what
belonged to the necessities and conveniences of Scholars,
and therefore have accommodated them accordingly ;
principally in providing them the patronages of many good
Benefices, whereby the Fellows of those Colleges are plenti-
fully maintained, after their leaving of the University.

Of the Colleges *University* is the oldest, *Pembroke* the
youngest, *Christ-church* the greatest, *Lincoln* (by many
reputed) the least, *Magdalen* the neatest, *Wadham* the most
uniform, *New-college* the strongest, and *Jesus college* (no 20
fault but its unhappiness) the poorest ; and if I knew
which was the richest, I would not tell, seeing concealment
in this kind is the safest. *New-college* is most proper for
Southern, *Exeter* for Western, *Queens* for Northern, *Brazen-
nose* for North-western men, *St. Johns* for *Londoners, Jesus*
for Welshmen ; and at other Colleges almost indifferently
for men of all Countries. *Merton* hath been most famous
for School-men, *Corpus Christi* (formerly called *Trilingue
Collegium*) for Linguists, *Christ-church* for Poets, *All-souls*
for Orators, *New-college* for Civilians, *Brazen-nose* for Dis- 30
putants, *Queens college* for Metaphysicians, *Exeter* for a late
series of *Regius Professor's ; Magdalen* for ancient, *St.*

Johns for modern Prelates : and all eminent in some one kind or other. And if any of these Colleges were transported into forreign parts, it would alter its *kind*, (or degree at least) and presently of a College *proceed* an University, as equal to most, and superior to many, *Academies* beyond the Seas.

Before I conclude with these Colleges, I must confess how much I was posed with a passage which I met with in the *Epistles* of *Erasmus*, writing to his familiar friend *Ludovicus Vives*, then residing in *Oxford, in collegio Apum*, in the College of Bees, according to his direction of his Letter : I knew all Colleges may metaphorically be termed the *Colleges of Bees*, wherein the industrious Scholers live under the rule of one Master : In which respect St. *Hierom* advised *Rusticus* the Monk to busie himself in making *Bee-hives*, that from thence he might learn, *Monasteriorum ordinem & Regiam disciplinam*, the order of Monasteries and discipline of Kingly government. But why any one College should be so signally called, and which it was, I was at a loss ; till at last seasonably satisfied that it was *Corpus Christi* : whereon no unpleasant story doth depend.

In the year 1630. the *Leads* over *Vives* his Study being decayed, were taken up and new cast, by which occasion the Stall was taken, and with it an incredible mass of Honey. But the *Bees*, as presaging their intended and imminent destruction (whereas they were never known to have swarmed before) did that Spring (to preserve their famous kind) send down a fair swarm into the Presidents Garden : The which in the year 1633. yielded two Swarms, one whereof pitched in the Garden for the President, the other they sent up as a new Colony into their old Habitation, there to continue the memory of this *mellifluous Doctor*, as the University styled him in a Letter to the Cardinal.

It seems these *Bees* were *Aborigines*, from the first

building of the Colledge, being called *Collegium Apum* in
the Founders Statutes, and so is *John Claymand*, the first
President thereof, saluted by *Erasmus*.

(*Oxford-shire*)

William Shakespeare

WILLIAM SHAKESPEARE was born at *Stratford* on *Avon*
in this County, in whom three eminent Poets may seem in
some sort to be compounded. 1. *Martial* in the *Warlike*
sound of his Sur-name, (whence some may conjecture him
of a *Military extraction*,) *Hasti-vibrans* or *Shake-speare*.
2. *Ovid*, the most *naturall* and *witty* of all Poets, and hence
it was that Queen *Elizabeth* coming into a Grammar-School
made this extemporary verse,

Persius *a Crab-staffe*, *Bawdy* Martial, Ovid *a fine Wag*.

3. *Plautus*, who was an exact Comædian, yet never any
Scholar, as our *Shake-speare* (if alive) would confess himself.
Adde to all these, that though his Genius generally was
jocular, and inclining him to *festivity*, yet he could (when
so disposed) be *solemn* and *serious*, as appears by his
Tragedies, so that *Heraclitus* himself (I mean if secret and
unseen) might afford to smile at his Comedies, they were so
merry, and *Democritus* scarce forbear to sigh at his Tragedies
they were so *mournfull*.

He was an eminent instance of the truth of that Rule,
Poeta non fit, sed nascitur, one is not *made* but *born* a Poet.
Indeed his Learning was very little, so that as *Cornish
diamonds* are not polished by any Lapidary, but are pointed
and smoothed even as they are taken out of the Earth, so
nature it self was all the *art* which was used upon him.

Many were the *wit-combates* betwixt him and *Ben Johnson*,
which two I behold like a *Spanish great Gallion*, and an

English man of War ; Master *Johnson* (like the former) was built far higher in Learning ; *Solid*, but *Slow* in his performances. *Shake-spear* with the *English-man of War*, lesser in *bulk*, but lighter in *sailing*, could turn with all tides, tack about and take advantage of all winds, by the quickness of his Wit and Invention. He died *Anno Domini* 16[16], and was buried at *Stratford* upon *Avon*, the Town of his Nativity.

(*Warwick-shire*)

Philemon Holland

PHILEMON HOLLAND, where born, is to me unknown, was bred in *Trinity-colledge* in *Cambridge*, a *Doctor* in *Physick*, and fixed himself in *Coventry*. He was the *Translator Generall* in his Age, so that those Books alone of his *Turning* into *English*, will make a *Country Gentleman* a competent library for *Historians*, in so much that one saith,

> Holland *with his Translations doth so fill us*,
> *He will not let* Suetonius *be* Tranquillus.

Indeed some decry all *Translators* as *Interlopers*, spoiling the Trade of Learning, which should be *driven* amongst Scholars alone. Such also alledge, that the best *Translations* are works, rather of *Industry* then *Judgement*, and (in easy Authors) of *Faithfulness*, rather then *Industry* ; That many be but *Bunglers*, forcing the meaning of the Authors, they translate, *picking the lock, when they cannot open it*.

But their Opinion resents too much of Envy, that such Gentlemen, who cannot repair to the Fountain, should be debard access to the Streame. Besides, it is unjust to charge *All*, with the faults of *some*, and a Distinction must be made amongst *Translators*, betwixt *Coblers* and *Workmen*, and our *Holland* had the true *knack* of Translating.

Many of these his Books he wrote with *One Pen*, whereon
he himself thus pleasantly versified.

> *With one sole pen I writ this Book,*
> *Made of a Grey Goose Quill.*
> *A Pen it was, when it I took,*
> *And a Pen I leave it still.*

This *Monumental Pen*, he solemnly kept and showed to my
reverend Tutor Doctor *Samuel Ward*. It seems he leaned
very lightly on the *Neb* thereof, though weightily enough,
in an other sense, performing not slightly, but solidly, what
he undertook.

But what commendeth him most to the Praise of Posterity, is his Translating *Camdens Britannia*, a *Translation*
more then a *Translation*, with many excellent Additions,
not found in the *Latine*, done *fifty* years since in Master
Camdens life time, not onely with his knowledge and consent, but also, no doubt, by his desire and help. Yet such
additions (discoverable in the former part with Asterisks
in the Margent) with some *Antiquaries* obtain not equal
Authenticalness with the rest. This eminent *Translator*
was Translated to a better life, *Anno Dom.* 16[37].

(Warwick-shire)

Roger Ascham

ROGER ASCHAM was born at *Kirby-weik* in this *County*,
and bred in Saint *Johns-Colledge* in *Cambridge*, under
Doctor *Medcalfe*, that good Governour, who *whet-stone-like*,
though dull in himself, by his encouragement, *set an edge*
on most excellent wits in that foundation. Indeed *Ascham*
came to *Cambridge* just at the *dawning* of learning, and
staid therein till the *bright-day* thereof, his own endeavours
contributing much *light* thereunto. He was *Oratour* and
Greek-Professour in the University, (places of some *sympathy*, which have often met in the same person,) and in

the beginning of the raign of Queen *Mary*, within *three* days, wrote letters to *fourty seven* severall Princes, whereof the meanest was a *Cardinal.* He travailed into *Germany*, and there contracted familiarity with *John Sturmius* and other learned men, and after his return was a kind of teacher to the Lady *Elizabeth*, to whom (after she was *Queen*) he became her *Secretary for her Latine letters.*

In a word, he was an *Honest man* and a *good Shooter* ; Archery (whereof he wrote a book called τοξόφιλος) being his onely *exercise* in his *youth*, which in his old age he *exchanged* for a worse *pastime*, neither so *healthfull* for his *body*, nor *profitable* for his *purse*, I mean *Cock-fighting*, and thereby (being neither greedy to get, nor carefull to keep money) he much impaired his estate.

He had a facile and fluent Latine-style, (not like those, who, counting *obscurity* to be *elegancy*, weed out all the hard words they meet in Authors,) witness his *Epistles*, which some say are the only Latine ones extant of any English-man, and if so, the more the pity. What *loads* have we of *letters* from forraign Pens, as if no Author were compleat without those necessary appurtenances ? whilst surely our English-men write, (though not so many,) as good as any other Nation. In a word, his τοξόφιλος is accounted a good book for *Young-men*, his *School-master* for *Old-men*, his *Epistles* for *all men*, set out after his death, which happened *Anno Dom.* 1568. *December* 30. in the 53 year of his Age, and he was buried in Saint *Sepulchers* in *London.*

(*York-shire*)

Sir Henry Saville

SIR HENRY SAVILL Knight, was born at *Bradley*, in the Parish of *Hallifax* in this *County*, of antient and worshipfull extraction. *He* was bred in *Oxford*, and at last became

Warden of *Merton-colledge* and also *Provost* of *Eaton*. Thus this skilfull *Gardiner* had at the same time a *Nurcery* of young *Plants*, and an *Orchard* of grown *Trees*, both flourishing under his carefull inspection.

This worthy *Knight* carefully collected the best Copies of Saint *Chrisostome*, and imployed Learned men to transcribe and make *Annotations* on them, which done, he fairly set it forth, on his own cost, in a most beautifull *Edition* ; a *burden* which he underwent without stooping under it, though the weight thereof would have broken 10 the back of an ordinary person. But the *Papists* at *Paris* had their *Emissaries* in *England*, who surrepticiously procured this *Knights* learned Labours, and sent them over weekly by the *Post* into *France*, *Schedatim* sheet by sheet, as here they passed the *Press*. Then *Fronto Duceus* (a French *Cardinall* as I take it) caused them to be Printed there with *implicite faith* and *blind obedience*, letter for letter as he received them out of *England*, onely joyning thereunto a *Latine translation* and some other inconsiderable Additions. Thus *two* Editions of Saint *Chrisostome* did 20 together run a race in the world, which should get the *speed* of the other in publique sale and acceptance. Sir *Henry* his *Edition* started first by the advantage of some Months. But the *Parisian Edition* came up close to it, and advantaged with the Latine Translation (though dearer of price) out-stript it in quickness of Sale, but of late the *Savilian Chrisostome* hath much mended its pace, so that very few are left of the whole Impression.

Sir *Henry* left one onely *Daughter* richly married to Sir *William Sidley* of *Kent* Baronet. He dyed at *Eaton*, where 30 he lyeth buried under a Monument with this Inscription *Hic jacent Ossa & Cineres* Henrici Savill *sub spe certa resurrectionis, natus apud* Bradley *juxta* Halifax *in Comitatu* Ebor, Anno Domini 1549. *ultimo die mensis* Novembris,

Obiit in Collegio Etonensi Anno Domini 1621. xix *die mensis* Februarii.

It must not be forgotten, that he was a most excellent Mathematician, witness his learned Lectures on *Euclid*. Yet once casually happening into the Company of Master *Briggs* of *Cambridge*, upon a learned encounter betwixt them, Master *Briggs* demonstrated a truth, besides (if not against) the judgment of Sir *Henry*, wherewith that worthy Knight was so highly affected, that he chose him one of his
10 Mathematick Professors in *Oxford*, wherein he founded *two* allowing a liberall sallary unto them.

(*York-shire*)

George Herbert

GEORGE HERBERT was born at *Montgomery Castle*, younger Brother to *Edward* Lord *Herbert* (of whom immediately) bred Fellow of *Trinity Colledge* in *Cambridge*, and Orator of the *University*, where he made a speech no less learned than the occasion was welcome, of the return of Prince *Charles* out of *Spain*.

He was none of the Nobles of *Tekoa*, who at the building
20 of *Jerusalem put not their necks to the work of the Lord* ; but waving worldly preferment, chose serving at Gods Altar before State employment. So pious his life, that he was a copy of primitive, he might be a pattern of Sanctity to posterity, to testifie his independency on all others, he never mentioned the name of *Jesus Christ*, but with this addition, *My Master*. Next God the Word, he loved the Word of God, being heard often to protest, That he *would not part with one leaf thereof for the whole world*.

Remarkable his conformity to Church-Discipline, where-
30 by he drew the greater part of his Parishioners to accompany him daily in the publick celebration of Divine Service. Yet had he (because not desiring) no higher preferment

than the Benefice of *Bemmerton* nigh *Salisbury* (where he
built a fair house for his Successor) and the Prebend of
Leighton (founded in the Cathedral of *Lincoln*) where he
built a fair Church, with the assistance of some few Friends
free Offerings.   When a Friend on his death bed went about
to comfort him with the remembrance thereof, as an
especial good work, he returned, *It is a good work if sprinkled
with the Blood of Christ*.   But his Church (that unimitable
piece of Poetry) may out-last this in structure.   His death
hapned *Anno Dom.* 163[3].   10

(Wales—Montgomery-shire)

NOTES

THE HOLY STATE

FULLER divides *The Holy State* into five books, the first dealing with the family—' The Good Wife ', ' The Good Husband ', &c. ; the second with miscellaneous characters ; the third with general topics such as ' Anger ', ' Fame ', ' Books ' ; the fourth with miscellaneous characters ; the fifth (*The Profane State*) with unrighteous characters.

The Holy State went to a second edition in 1648, a third in 1652, a fourth in 1663.

This ' leakage of [Fuller's] soul ' on the way to the *Church History* follows a literary fashion of his day. The invention of the *Character* is attributed to the Greek writer, Theophrastus (B.C. 372–287). The *Characters of Virtues and Vices* (1608) by Joseph Hall is the earliest important example in English. Among Fuller's notable predecessors in this kind are Sir Thomas Overbury, *Characters or Witty Descriptions of the Properties of Sundry Persons* (1614) ; Nicholas Breton, *Characters upon Essays, Moral and Divine* (1615) and *The Good and the Bad or Descriptions of the Worthies and Unworthies of this Age. Where the Best may see their Graces, and the Worst discern their Baseness* (1616) ; and John Earle, *Micro-cosmographie or A Piece of the World Discovered in Essays and Characters* (1628). The purpose of the Theophrastan *Character*—to portray types, to compose in a single harmonious picture the characteristics of a class—is reflected in the foregoing subtitles. ' To square out a character by our English levell ', wrote Overbury, ' it is a picture (reall or personall) quaintly drawne, in various colours, all of them heightened by one shadowing. It is a quicke and soft touch of many strings, all shutting up in one musicall close : it is wits descant upon any plaine song ' (' What a Character is ', *Characters or Witty Descriptions*).

Fuller's Characters are more diffuse and formless than the artful productions of Overbury and Earle, which aim at being succinct, epigrammatic, and symmetrical ; but they are no less pleasant reading.

PAGE **37**, l. 19. *Wise Solon.* Herodotus, lib. i, cap. xxx.

PAGE **39**, l. 15. *Pythis.* Plutarch, *de Virtut. Mulierum, exemplo ultimo.*

PAGE **40**, l. 9. *one calls.* Bacon, *Life of Henry VII*, ed. 1641, p. 74.

PAGE **42**, l. 17. *Primus ab infusis, etc.*

The Dove, Columba, first the Tidings brought
To Noah's ark, *The Waters now subside !*
Columbus, too, what some had vainly sought,
Was he who first the Western World descried.

(Quoted from James Nichols, *The Holy State*, Lond. 1841, p. 122.)

PAGE **43**, l. 29. *the Six Articles* (33 Henry VIII) enjoined (1) belief in the real presence of Christ in the Eucharist ; (2) the sufficiency of communion in one kind ; (3) the celibacy of the priests ; (4) the obligation of vows of chastity ; (5) the expediency of private masses ; and (6) the necessity of auricular confession.

PAGE **46**, l. 29. *Caboverd*, Cape de Verd.

PAGE **48**, l. 28. *Aurum Tholosanum*. The pillage of the temple of Tolosanum (Toulouse) by the Romans in 106 B.C. gave rise to the expression *Aurum Tolosanum*—ill-gotten gains.

PAGE **49**, l. 2. *the waining*, &c., the decline of the power of Spain. See p. 109, l. 29.

l. 13. *Caravall*, or *carvel*, a light vessel without decks and with a square poop.

PAGE **52**, l. 16. *Hevenninghams*, or Effinghams.

PAGE **55**, l. 22. Genesis xxxii. 25.

PAGE **56**, l. 2. Matthew v. 22.

l. 24. Exodus xvi. 24.

l. 26. Ephesians iv. 26.

PAGE **58**, l. 20. *Dedicatory epistle*. Fuller himself was the most prolific and ingenious of dedicators (see notes on the *Pisgah-sight* and the *Church History*). Dr. Johnson's opinion of dedications will serve to counterbalance Fuller's : ' I do not myself think that a man should say in a dedication what he could not say in a history. However, allowance should be made ; for there is a great difference. The known style of a dedication is flattery : it professes to flatter. There is the same difference between what a man says in a dedication, and what he says in a history, as between a lawyer's pleading a cause, and reporting it.' (Boswell, ed. G. B. Hill, vol. v, pp. 285-6.)

PAGE **59**, l. 7. *Pro tantorum*, &c., so far from being rewarded for his great labours, was scarcely pardoned for them.

l. 12. *our worthy English Knight*, Sir Henry Savile. For Fuller's account of him, see p. 190. Savile's edition of Chrysostom is said to have cost the editor £8,000. According to Hallam (*Literature of Europe*, iii. 10, 11), it was ' the first work of learning, on a great scale, published in England '.

PAGE **60**, l. 7. *Multi mei*, &c. Erasmus, in *Praefatio in*

tertiam seriem Hieron. Operum, iv, p. 408 : Many like me suffer
from the disease of not knowing how to write and yet being
unable to keep from writing.

PAGE **61,** l. 3. *a good Time-server.* Fuller's own life conformed with these precepts. His immunity from persecution,
his peaceful occupation of successive curacies while his fellow-
divines were suffering, exposed him to suspicion. In his *Animadversions*, Heylin made the charge that Fuller ' complied with
the times '. Thomas Hearne (Diary, 24 August, 1720, quoted
by Bailey, *Life*, p. 449) says of the anonymous *Life* : ' A great
character of the Dr. is in it. Yet he was certainly a Trimmer.'
In his *Appeal of Injured Innocence*, Fuller distinguishes between
an improper and a proper compliance with the times. It is
permissible, he contends, for a man to refrain ' (though not
without secret sorrow) *from some Laudable Act* which he heartily
desireth, but dares not doe, as visibly destructive to his *Person
and Estate*, being prohibited by the Predominant Powers : In
such a case, a man may, to use the Apostle's phrase, διὰ τὴν
ἐνεστῶσαν ἀνάγκην, *for the present necessity* (1 Cor. vii. 26) omit
many things Pleasing to, but not Commanded by, that God
who preferreth Mercy before Sacrifice. . . .

' I have Endevoured to steer my Carriage by the Compass
aforesaid ; and my main Motive thereunto was, that I might
enjoy the Benefit of my *Ministry*, the bare using whereof,
is the greatest Advancement I am capable of in this
Life. . . .

' But it will be objected against me, that it is suspicious (at
the least) that I have *Bribed* the *Times* with some base Compliance with them, because they have reflected so favorably
upon me. Otherwise, how cometh it to pass, that *my fleece*, like
Gideons, is *dry*, when the rest of my *Brethren* of the *same party*
are *wet* with their own Tears ? . . .

' I answer first, I impute this Peaceableness I enjoy, to Gods
undeserved Goodness on my Unworthiness. . . .

' Next to the fountain of Gods Goodness, I ascribe my Liberty
of Preaching to the *Favour* of some *Great* Friends God hath
raised up for me. It was not a Childish answer, though the
answer of a Child to his Father, taxing him for being Proud
of his New *Coat, I am glad,* (said he) *but not proud of it !* . . .

' All I will add is this, that . . . I have not by my *Pen*, or
Practice to my knowledge done anything *Unworthily* to the
betraying of the Interest of the Church of *England*.'

PAGE **62,** l. 2. *the Book of Martyrs.* For the vivid impression
made upon Fuller, as a child, by the pictures in the *Book of
Martyrs*, see p. 84. Fuller's life of Fox, in *Abel Redevivus*, will

be found on pp. 105 ff. Fuller desired that his Church History
' should behave itself to [the] *Book of Martyrs*, as a *Lieutenant*
to its *Captain*, onely to supply his place in his absence, to be
supplemental thereunto, in such matters of moment which
have escaped his observation' (*Church History*, Bk. V, p. 231).

PAGE **64,** l. 3.   *scandalous aspersions.* In Nicholas Sanders'
de Origine ac Progressu Schismatis Anglicani (which formed the
basis of every Roman Catholic history of the English Reformation) is the story that Anne Boleyn was King Henry's own
daughter.

PAGE **65,** l. 7.   *Mother*, an hysterical malady.

> ' O, how this Mother swells up toward my heart ! '
> > > Shakespeare, *Lear*, II. iv. 56.

> ' The Mother is a pestilent, wilful, troublesome sickness.'
> > > Middleton, *Michaelmas Term*, III. i.

PAGE **66,** l. 24.   Fuller refers to the fact that the coinage was
restored to its par value in the reign of Queen Elizabeth.

PAGE **74,** l. 7.   Cf. Overbury's *Character* of 'A Roaring Boy'.
' His life is a meere counterfet patent, which neverthelesse makes
many a countrey justice tremble. . . .   He sends challenges by
word of mouth : for he protests (as he is a gentleman and
brother of the sword) he can neither write nor read.   He hath
runne through divers parcels of land, and great houses, beside
both the counters. . . .   He cheats young guls that are newly
come to towne ; and when the keeper of the Ordinary blames
him for it, he answers him in his owne profession, that a *wood-
cocke* must be pluckt ere he be drest.'

PAGE **75,** l. 13.   *battle*, fatten.

l. 19.   *punto*, punctilio.

PAGE **76,** l. 25.   Cf. *Church History, Book* VI, *section* IV :
' Once being at dice, [King Henry] played with Sir *Miles Pat-
ridge* (staking an hundred pounds against them) for *Jesus Bells*,
hanging in a Steeple not farre from *S. Paul's* in *London*, and
as great, and tuneable as any in the City, and lost them at
a cast.'

PAGE **78,** l. 22.   *Presidents*, precedents.

PAGE **80.**   GOOD THOUGHTS IN BAD TIMES

Good Thoughts in Bad Times was composed during Fuller's
residence in Exeter as chaplain in the household of the infant
princess, Henrietta Anne.   According to J. E. Bailey, *Life*,
p. 351, it was ' the first book printed in the city '.   In his
dedication, Fuller terms it ' the first-fruits of Exeter press '.
The book is divided into ' Personal Meditations ', ' Scripture
Observations ', ' Historical Applications ' and ' Mixt Contem-

plations '. Fuller dedicated it to his patroness, Lady Dalkeith, ' Lady Governess to her Highness, the Princess Henrietta '.

PAGE 81, l. 6.   *Nabuchadnezars Image*.   Daniel iii. 1.

l. 27.   *Man goeth*, &c.   Eccles. xii. 5.

PAGE 82, l. 27.   *Take double Money*.   Genesis xliii. 12.

PAGE 84, l. 15.   *fiery Fournace*.   Daniel iii. 27.

l. 19.   *though the Lion*, &c.   A Spanish proverb.

PAGE 85, l. 5.   *Pisgah Top*.   Deuteronomy iii. 27.

l. 20.   *Murthering Pieces*, a common term at this time for cannon, reflecting the horror of the execution which they wrought.   Cf. *Hamlet* IV. v. 95.

> this,
> Like to a murdering-piece, in many places
> Gives me superfluous death.

PAGE 85.   GOOD THOUGHTS IN WORSE TIMES

The two years that had elapsed since the publication of *Good Thoughts in Bad Times* had been painful to Fuller. The King was in captivity; the use of the Liturgy had been forbidden in the churches. In 1647 Fuller found himself without employment and in debt. *Good Thoughts in Worse Times* reflects his melancholy mood. ' We have no more *house*-burnings, but many *heart*-burnings: and though outward bleeding be stanched, it is to be feared that the broken vein bleeds *inwards*, which is more dangerous.' It is significant that this little book appears without a dedication. ' Dedications', he observes, ' begin now-a-days to grow out of fashion.'

PAGE 86.   MIXT CONTEMPLATIONS IN BETTER TIMES

Mixt Contemplations in Better Times is dated Zion College, May 2, 1660,—as Bailey points out (*Life*, p. 667), ' the day after the reading of the King's letter to the Speaker, and the day before the proclaiming of the King '. It is dedicated ' to the truely honourable and most virtuous lady, the Lady Monck '.

PAGE 89.   A PISGAH-SIGHT OF PALESTINE

This work was undertaken immediately after Fuller's appointment as curate of Waltham. ' So soon as God's goodness gave me a fixt habitation, I composed my *Land of Canaan*, or *Pisgah-sight*.' It was entered on the Stationers' Register, April 15, 1649, as ' A Choragraphicall Comment on the history of the Bible or the description of Judea by Tho. Fuller, B.D.' The title finally chosen is anticipated in the heading of chapter xviii of his *Historie of the Holy Warre* (1639) : ' A Pisgah-sight, or Short survey of Palestine in general.' The 1650 folio of the

Pisgah-sight is illustrated with many quaintly drawn maps, representing not only the localities of Jewish history but also the events associated with them,—' Properties ' or ' History-pictures ', Fuller called them. With respect to the accuracy both of the maps and the text, Fuller thinks that ' a large and charitable latitude must still be allowed in a subject so hard and full of uncertainty '. He quaintly justifies his plea by the example of the Holy Ghost, who ' speaks not positively of distances of places, but with words of qualification. *About three-score furlongs from Jerusalem to Emmaus ; About five and twenty or thirty furlongs they had rowed on the sea ;* as if five in thirty made no considerable difference. If the same favour may be but allowed our scale of miles, I doubt not but it will acquit it self against all just exception.'

The *Pisgah-sight* is arranged in Fuller's favourite five-fold division—first, a prefatory description of Judea ; second, an account of the tribes ; third, an account of Jerusalem and the Temple ; fourth, of the surrounding nations ; fifth, a miscellany.

In addition to the general dedication to Esme Stuart, infant son of James, Duke of Richmond and Lennox, a few lines of which Lamb quotes in his ' Specimens ' (see p. 14), the remaining books are dedicated respectively to Henry, Lord Beauchamp ; to Lord John Rosse, son of the Earl of Rutland ; to Francis Lord Russell, son of the Earl of Bedford (the two patrons last named being each in his twelfth year) ; and to John Lord Burghley, infant son of the Earl of Exeter. In the dedication of the fifth book to Lord Burghley, Fuller describes himself as ' planting a Nursery of Patrons, all Noble, but of different years, a Babe, a Child, two Youths of several date, and a Man, (having as a Scale of Miles in my Maps, a Scale of Ages in my Honourable Patrons), hoping so always to have one or more in full power to protect my endeavours '.

PAGE **90**, l. 9.   *There is not amongst us,* 1 Kings v. 6.

l. 16.   *the Harvest of the River,* Isaiah xxiii. 3.

l. 19.   *I am of perfect Beauty,* Ezekiel xxvii. 3.

PAGE **91**, l. 21.   *Jerusalem is turned,* Ezekiel xxvi. 2.

l. 25.   *to stain the pride of her glory,* Isaiah xxiii. 9.

l. 28.   *two maritime expressions,* Ezekiel xxvi. 3, and xxvii. 26.

PAGE **92**, l. 4.   *served a great service,* Ezekiel xxix. 18.

l. 12.   *the spoile of the Land of Egypt,* Ezekiel xxix. 19.

l. 30.   *to sing as an harlot,* Isaiah xxiii. 15.

PAGE **93**, l. 22.   *clothed in purple,* St. Luke xvi. 19.

PAGE **94**, l. 24.   *Chorazin and Bethsaida,* St. Matthew xi. 21.

PAGE 95, l. 33.   *the sound of an Ax*, 1 Kings vi. 7.

PAGE 96, l. 7.   *How could these things be*, St. John iii. 9.

l. 22.   According to the legend, Solomon obtained through the agency of Ashmedai the *Shamir*, either a worm or an exceedingly hard stone, which hewed or cut with perfect ease the granite, marble, and glass used in building the Temple. Its mere touch cleft the hardest substance. In size the *Shamir* was no larger than a grain. It had been preserved since the creation of the world.

PAGE 97, l. 1.   *they brake down the carved work.* Psalm lxxiv. 6.

PAGE 101.   ABEL REDEVIVUS

Abel Redevivus comprises one hundred and seven biographies, of which only seven are by Fuller. In addition to the two reprinted in this book, Fuller is responsible for the biographies of Berengarius, Hus, Cranmer, Perkins, and Junius. ' Providence so ordereth it,' Fuller explains in the Epistle to the Reader, ' that out of the ashes of dead Saints, many living ones doe spring and sprout, by following the pious precedents of such godly persons deceased. This was a maine motive of publishing the ensuing Treatise, to furnish our present Age with a Magazeen of religious patterns for their Imitation.'

PAGE 102, l. 6.   *a Troope shall overcome him.*   Genesis xlix. 19.

PAGE 104, l. 27.   *We went through fire.*   Psalm lxvi. 12.

PAGE 105, l. 3.   *Away with such a fellow.*   Acts xxii. 22.

PAGE 111.   THE CHURCH HISTORY

The Church History had been long in contemplation. In *The Holy State* (1642) Fuller announced his intention to write ' the Ecclesiastical History from Christs time to our dayes ' (see p. 34). If *The Holy State* was ' the leakage of his soul ' (p. 34, l. 14) on the way to the *Church History*, the *Pisgah-sight* (as he explains in *The Appeal of Injured Innocence*) was ' the clearing of the floor or foundation ' for that great edifice. During the thirteen years ensuing upon the publication of *The Holy State*, his admirers frequently reminded him of his promise and urged the completion of the work.

Fuller had been advised (for reasons of policy) against extending his history beyond the death of King James. When, after long hesitation, he decided to protract it into his own times, he cleared the way with characteristic caution. ' I know ', he writes in the dedicatory epistle of the tenth book to Robert, Lord Bruce, son of the first Earl of Elgin, that ' *Machiavel* was wont to say, That *he who undertakes to Write a History, must be of no Religion* : if so, *he* himself was the best

qualified of any in *his Age* to be a *good Historian.* But, I believe, his *meaning* was much better than his *words,* intending
therein, That a *Writer of Histories must not discover his inclination in Religion to the prejudice of Truth* : *Levi-like,* who said
to his *Father* and *Mother, I have not seen them,* owning no
acquaintance of any *Relations.* This I have endeavoured to my
utmost in *this Book* ; knowing, as *that Oyle* is adjudged *the best*
that hath *no tast at all;* so *that Historian* is preferred, who hath
the *least Tangue* of *partial Reflections.* However, some *Candour
of course* is due to such *Historians,* (wherein the *Courtesie* not
so great in *giving* as the *Injury* in *detaining* it) which *run the
Chiding* of these *present Times* in hope that *after-Ages* may
excuse them. And I am confident that these *my Labours* shall
finde the same *favour* (which may be in *meer men,* should be in
all gentlemen, must be in *true Christians*) the rather because *this
Booke* appeareth *Patronized* by a *Dedication* to *Your Honour.*'

Fuller's account of ' Mr. John Dod ' (pp. 136–8) exemplifies
alike his impartiality and his skill in implication, in dealing
with delicate matters.

The *Church History* is initially dedicated to the five-year-old
Esme Stuart, Duke of Richmond, to whom Fuller had dedicated the *Pisgah-sight.* Not less than eighty-four other patrons
and patronesses receive dedications in the prefatory epistles to
the successive ' books ', ' centuries ' and ' sections ' of the
Church History. As a collector of patrons in an age when
patron-hunting had become a fine art, Fuller stands easily
primus inter pares.

PAGE **114,** l. 17. *saith Bede,* in *Eccles. Hist.,* lib. ii, cap. 9.

PAGE **116,** l. 17. *to him that sacrificeth,* Ecclesiastes ix. 2.

l. 18. *Judgement beginneth,* 1 Peter iv. 17.

l. 26. *Mans life.* Bede, *Eccles. Hist.,* lib. ii, cap. 13.

PAGE **118,** l. 31. *Cunctum,* &c. Passing the whole time of
his life in one monastery.

PAGE **119,** l. 2. *she departed not,* St. Luke ii. 37.

PAGE **120,** l. 19. *that Beast, cannot overcome,* Revelation xi. 7.

PAGE **121,** l. 3. *Leland,* John (1506–1552), the antiquary. He
was the first to write a life of Chaucer, and it was first printed in
1709, in his *Commentarii de Scriptoribus Britannicis,* edited by
A. Hall, vol. ii, pp. 419–26. It was accessible to Fuller only
in manuscript. ' *Algerum* ' is Fuller's mistake for ' *Aligerum* '.

l. 12. *Verstegan,* in his *Restitution of Decayed Intelligence,*
1605, p. 203.

PAGE **122,** l. 1. *a modern Author,* Sir George Buck, in his
History of the Life and Reigne of Richard The Third (1646), Book
iii, p. 75. ' So much gall and envy is thrown upon King

Richard's story, as cannot possibly fall into the stile of an
ingenuous and charitable pen ; all his virtue is by a malitious
Alchymy subtracted into crimes. . . . They have yet a more
captious and subtle calumny, reproching the casting of his
eyes, motions of his fingers, manner of his gesture, and his other
naturall actions. . . . Nay, they will dissect his very sleepes, to
find prodigious dreames and bugbears . . . their envy is borne
with him from his mother's wombe, and delivers him into the
world with a strange prodigy of Teeth ; although (I am perswaded) neither Doctor Morton, nor Sir Thomas Moore ever
spake with the Dutchesse his Mother, or her Midwife about the
matter. But if true ; it importeth no reason why those early
and natalitious teeth should presage such horrour and guilt to
his birth.'

PAGE **125,** l. 9. *Secundum usum Sarum,* according to the
Sarum use—the order of divine service used in the diocese of
Salisbury from the eleventh century to the Reformation.

l. 17. *learned Apologie.* While Bishop of Salisbury (1560–71)
Jewel issued his *Apologia pro Ecclesia Anglicana,* 1562.

PAGE **130,** l. 12. *one (then a great wit . . .),* Joseph Hall
(1574–1656), fellow of Emmanuel College, Cambridge, Bishop
of Exeter 1627–41, and Bishop of Norwich 1641–7.

PAGE **143.** THE APPEAL OF INJURED INNOCENCE

Dr. Peter Heylyn, whose ' animadversions ' against Fuller's
Church History occasioned the *Appeal,* was an Oxford man, a
staunch Royalist, and an acrimonious controversialist. *Micro-
cosmos, or a Description of the Great World* (1621), and a *History
of that most famous Saint and Souldier of Christ Jesus, St.
George of Cappadocia : Asserted from the Fictions of the Middle
Ages of the Church and opposition of the present* (1631), established his reputation. His life of Laud (of whom he was a
vehement supporter) appeared under the title of *Cyprianus
Anglicus* in 1668, after the controversy with Fuller.

Heylyn is said himself to have intended a history of the
Church of England since the Reformation. Thwarted by the
difficulties in which he was involved upon the collapse of
the Royalist cause, it is possible that he was jealous of Fuller's
success. Minor sources of irritation were Fuller's sceptical jests,
in the *Pisgah-sight* and the *Church History,* about the legends of
St. George ; the doubt which Fuller ventured to express (albeit
with characteristic mildness) of Oxford's claim to greater antiquity than Cambridge's, and Fuller's remark (surely innocent
enough) that seventeen weeks of residence at Lincoln College
cost him ' more than seventeen years in Cambridge '. These
small offences Heylyn does not fail to catalogue, in the massive

attack which, after four years of deliberation, he made upon the *Church History*. His *Examen Historicum : or a Discovery and Examination of the Mistakes, Falsities, and Defects in some Modern Histories* (1659), consists of two parts, the first comprising the ' necessary animadversions ' against Fuller's *Church History*, the second dealing with a history of the Stuarts by William Sanderson. Heylyn's attack ranges from a catalogue of trivial inaccuracies and ineptitudes to general condemnation of manner and matter—irrelevance, a jesting spirit that does not ' become the gravity of a Church-historian ', and a ' continual vein of Puritanism '.

In the *Appeal* (1659) Fuller admits that there are inaccuracies in his *History* (which, he reminds the reader, is after all but ' endeavoured ') ; justifies his jests with the plea that good stories may be found in the writings of the gravest authors ; and in answer to Heylyn's more serious charges, reasserts both his loyalty to the Church and the propriety of his preserving an impartial attitude as a historian. The charity and sweetness of temper reflected in the brief selections here printed are sustained throughout the *Appeal*.

PAGE **144,** l. 22. *his Mess*, Genesis xliii. 44.

PAGE **145,** l. 7. *paradigmatize*, to set forth as an example.

PAGE **146,** l. 2. *Of making many Books*, Ecclesiastes xii. 12.

l. 22. *yet one History,—The Worthies*. See p. 149 and note.

PAGE **148,** l. 21. *Onesimus*, Philemon, vv. 10–15.

PAGE **149.** THE WORTHIES OF ENGLAND

Fuller began *The Worthies* as early as 1644, when he was chaplain in the field to Lord Hopton. The anonymous *Life* (see pp. 1–2) gives a lively picture of his assiduity in collecting materials. The book was nearing completion in 1655 and is recorded as ' ready to be launched ' in 1659 (see p. 146, l. 24) ; but publication was delayed by the controversy with Dr. Heylyn. The ' five ends ' which Fuller set for himself are engagingly expounded in ' The Design of the Work ' (see pp. 150–2). In Chapter XXIV, entitled ' Exceptions against the style and matter of the author prevented ', Fuller anticipates the criticism that his biographies are overloaded with ' Scripture observations and reflections in divinity '. He confesses ' to have (I will not say a *partiality*) but an *affection* to the expressions of, and excursions into, my own Calling. Secondly, I plead Conscience, that, seeing some may Cavil this Work to be a Deviation from my function (and I my self perchance sensible of some truth therein), I will watch and catch all opportunity to make a fair regresse to my profession '.

Fuller died on 16 August, 1661, leaving his work incomplete. It was hurried through the press and appeared (with a dedication to King Charles from the pen of Fuller's son John) early in the following year. It was on sale by 10 February 1661/2, when Pepys found a copy on a stall in Paul's churchyard—'the first time that I ever saw it'.

PAGE **151,** l. 26. John xii. 18.

PAGE **152,** l. 9. *and now when shall I provide*, Genesis xxx. 30.

PAGE **154,** ll. 6–7. *The History of the University of Cambridge since the Conquest* (1655), appended to the *Church History*.

l. 16. *our great Antiquary*, Camden, in his *Britannia* (Cheshire).

l. 18. *Arte militari*, &c., he served with distinction in France, his courage finding a way through every difficulty.

PAGE **156,** l. 1. *The History of Great Britaine* (1611).

PAGE **159,** l. 3. *Hundreth Good Pointes of Husbandrie* (1557) ; *Hundreth Poyntes of Good Husserie* (1558) ; *Five Hundreth Pointes of Good Husbandry united to as many of Good Huswifery* (1573) : crude didactic verse, many times reprinted, and the source of many proverbial sayings still current.

l. 9. *Columella* (fl. 50 A. D.), the chief Latin writer on agriculture. His *De Re Rustica* is in twelve books, of which one— Book x, De Cultu Hortorum—is in verse.

l. 10. *the Poet*, Ovid. *Ars. Amat.* ii. 548.

PAGE **160,** l. 6. His *Divine Emblems* (1635) has engravings by William Marshall.

l. 8. Andrea Alciati (1492–1550), Italian jurist and poet, is the most famous of the Emblem-writers.

PAGE **162,** l. 27. *excursions into Poetry.* John Davies of Hereford (1565–1618) is best known for his 'Picture of an Happy Man' in *The Muse's Sacrifice* (1612). His poems are reprinted in *The Chertsey Worthies Library* (1873). He is not to be confused with his greater contemporary, Sir John Davies, author of *Nosce Teipsum*.

PAGE **164,** l. 17. The collections of Sir Robert Cotton became the property of the Nation in 1702, and in 1753 a nucleus of the library of the British Museum.

PAGE **168,** l. 9. *my Authour*, John Bale, in his *Scriptorum Illustrium maioris Britanniæ Catalogus* (1559), Cent. viii. Num. lxxxvii (p. 680) : 'from being a quarrelsome solicitor became the gentlest of Christ's apostles'.

PAGE **170,** l. 17. *fourth generation.* Job xlii. 16.

PAGE **178,** l. 26. *my Author*, Camden, in his *Elizabeth, in anno 1598* : 'he suffered the usual fate of poets in having a continual struggle with poverty'.

PAGE **182,** l. 15. *Sir John Oldcastle,* so named in the early chronicle play, *The Famous Victories of Henry V.* That Shakespeare first called the fat knight of his *Henry IV* Sir John Oldcastle is indicated by the prince's pun when addressing Falstaff as 'my old lad of the castle' (*1 Henry IV*, I. ii. 47). Tradition has it that descendants of the actual Sir John Oldcastle compelled Shakespeare to change the name and to make the disclaimer in the epilogue to *2 Henry IV* : 'Oldcastle died a martyr, and this is not the man.' In spite of the change, the name of Oldcastle clung to the part. Nathaniel Field (*Amends for Ladies,* 1618), referring to *1 Henry IV*, v. i. 128–45, asks

> Did you never see
> The Play where the fat Knight, hight *Old-castle,*
> Did tell you truly what this honor was ?

PAGE **191,** l. 5. See p. 59, l. 12, note.

PAGE **192,** l. 10. *Mathematick Professors in Oxford.* He founded the two professorships now called the Savilian Professorship of Astronomy and the Savilian Professorship of Geometry.

l. 14. *of whom immediately.* In *The Worthies* the account of Lord Herbert of Cherbury follows the passage here quoted about George Herbert.

l. 19. *the Nobles of Tekoa,* Nehemiah iii. 5.

PAGE **193,** l. 8. *The Temple, or Sacred Poems and Private Ejaculations* (1634).

PRINTED IN ENGLAND AT THE UNIVERSITY PRESS OXFORD
BY JOHN JOHNSON PRINTER TO THE UNIVERSITY

Some Oxford Anthologies

of

ENGLISH LITERATURE

❡ *Verse Anthologies*

The Oxford Book of English Verse, edited by SIR ARTHUR QUILLER-COUCH. Pp. 1,096. 8s. 6d. net. On India paper, 10s. net.

The English Parnassus, by W. MACNEILE DIXON and H. J. C. GRIERSON. An anthology of longer poems. Pp. 784. 6s. 6d. net.

England's Parnassus, compiled by R. ALLOT, 1600; edited by C. CRAWFORD. Pp. 604. 8s. 6d. net. On India paper, 10s. 6d. net.

Palgrave's Golden Treasury, with Additional Poems, edited with introduction and notes by C. B. WHEELER. Pp. 756. 4s. Text only, 2s. net. *World's Classics*, 133.

A Book of Verse for Boys and Girls, compiled by J. C. SMITH. Pp. 536. 4s. 6d. Separately, in paper, and in cloth boards: I, pp. 64, 8d., 1s.; II, pp. 160, 1s. 4d., 1s .8d.; III, pp. 312, 2s. 6d., 3s.

A Book of Verse from Langland to Kipling, compiled by J. C. SMITH. Pp. 298. 3s. 6d.

Poems of Action, selected by V. H. COLLINS. Pp. 160. 2s. With notes, 3s.

Poems of Action, Second Series, selected by V. H. COLLINS and H. A. TREBLE. Pp. 189. 2s.

Lyra Historica: *Poems of English History*, selected by M. E. WINDSOR and J. TURRAL. Annotated. Pp. 224. 3s. Also separately: I, A. D. 61–1381, 1s. 3d. II, 1388–1641, 1s. 3d III, 1644–1910, 1s. 6d.

A Book of Ballads, selected by J. C. SMITH and G. SOUTAR. Annotated. Pp. 200. 2s. 6d.

October 1928

Some Oxford Anthologies of

Stories in Verse, selected by V. H. COLLINS. Pp. 172. 2s.

Poems of Home and Overseas, compiled by CHARLES WILLIAMS and V. H. COLLINS. Pp. 160. 3s.

A Book of Modern Verse, compiled by J. C. SMITH. Pp. 64. 1s. Library Edition, 2s. 6d. net.

A Book of Longer Modern Verse, edited by E. A. PARKER. Pp. 152. 2s. Library Edition, 3s. 6d. net.

A Book of Victorian Narrative Verse, compiled by C. WILLIAMS. Pp. 337. 2s. 6d. Library Edition, 3s. 6d. net.

A Book of Victorian Verse, chiefly lyrical, edited with notes by V. H. COLLINS. Pp. 160. 2s. 6d.

Spoken Verse for Schools and Festivals, arranged by T. HENDERSON, with introductions by J. C. SMITH. I, Elementary, pp. 64. 1s. II, Advanced, pp. 96. 2s. The two parts together, 2s. 6d.

¶ Prose Anthologies and Readers

The Oxford Book of English Prose, chosen and edited by SIR ARTHUR QUILLER-COUCH. Pp. 1,112. 8s. 6d. net. On India paper, 10s. net.

English Prose from Mandeville to Ruskin, chosen by W. PEACOCK, with notes by T. BALSTON. Pp. 536. 3s. 6d. Text only, 2s. net. *World's Classics*, 45.

English Prose, Narrative, Descriptive, Dramatic (Malory to Stevenson), compiled by H. A. TREBLE. Pp. 522. 2s. net. *World's Classics*, 204.

English Prose from Bacon to Hardy, selected and edited by E. K. BROADUS and R. K. GORDON. Pp. 626. 6s. 6d. net.

English Essays from Bacon to Stevenson, chosen by W. PEACOCK, with notes by C. B. WHEELER. Pp. 700. 3s. 6d. Text only, 2s. net. *World's Classics*, 32.

A Book of English Essays, *1600–1900*, chosen by S. V. MAKOWER and B. H. BLACKWELL, with notes by A. F. SCHUSTER. Pp. 588. 3s. 6d. Text only, 2s. net. *World's Classics*, 172.

English Critical Essays of the XIXth Century, selected and edited with notes by E. D. JONES. Pp. 674. 3s. 6d. Text only, 2s. net. *World's Classics*, 206.

Modern English Essays from 'Mark Rutherford' to J. Middleton Murry, selected by H. S. MILFORD. Pp. 424. 2s. net. *World's Classics*, 280.

English Literature

Selected English Short Stories (XIXth Century),
First Series. Pp. 486. 2s. net.

Selected English Short Stories (XIXth and XXth
Centuries), Second Series. Edited with notes by H. S. MILFORD.
Pp. 516. 3s. Text only, 2s. net. *World's Classics,* 228.

Selected English Short Stories (XIXth and XXth
Centuries), Third Series. Pp. 507. 2s. net.

A Round of Tales, edited by N. HENRY and H A.
TREBLE. Pp. 192. 2s. Selections from Washington Irving,
Marryat, Hawthorne, E. A. Poe, Dickens, Ruskin, F. R. Stockton,
Bret Harte, Isabella Harwood, Thomas Hardy, 'Anthony Hope',
Sir Arthur Quiller-Couch, and Algernon Blackwood.

A Second Round of Tales, edited by N. HENRY and
H. A. TREBLE. Pp. 192. 2s. Selections from Washington Irving,
R. H. Barham, Hawthorne, E. A. Poe, Elizabeth Gaskell, Bret
Harte, Ambrose Bierce, Conan Doyle, G. K. Chesterton, Sir Arthur
Quiller-Couch, W. W. Jacobs.

Tales of Action, chosen by V. H. COLLINS and
H. A. TREBLE. Pp. 160. 2s. Selections from Scott, Southey,
E. J. Trelawny, E. A. Poe, Kinglake, Dickens, Kingsley, Sir
Walter Besant, R. L. Stevenson, Sir Arthur Conan Doyle.

Tales of Adventure and Imagination, edited by
H. A. TREBLE. Pp. 192. 2s.

The Clarendon Readers in Literature and Science,
edited by J. C. SMITH. A series of three illustrated volumes for use
in schools, 2s. 6d. each. I, pp. 312, with 38 illustrations. II, pp. 287,
with 30 illustrations. III, pp. 320, with 35 illustrations. 3s. 6d.

¶ Dramatic Anthologies and Readers

Specimens of the Elizabethan Drama from Lyly to
Shirley, edited by W. H. WILLIAMS. Pp. 584. 7s. 6d. net.

A Dramatic Reader, by A. R. HEADLAND and H. A.
TREBLE. A series of four volumes of graduated difficulty. I, pp.
112. 2s. II, pp. 112. 2s. III, pp. 176. 2s. 6d. IV, pp. 202. 3s.

English Texts for Schools

Select English Classics (' *Q' Classics*). A series with introductions by Sir Arthur Quiller-Couch. Fcap 8vo. 6d. each.

Oxford Plain Texts. Fcap 8vo, varying in price from 6d. to 1s. 6d. Nearly 100 of these texts have now been issued, including twenty-four of the plays of Shakespeare.

Annotated English Classics under the general editorship of C. B. Wheeler. Longer works in prose and verse, mostly complete, suitable for higher forms and Universities. This series, of which over 60 volumes have been issued, includes anthologies like Palgrave's Golden Treasury, pp. 756, and Peacock's English Essays, pp. 700. Prices from 10d. to 5s. net.

The Clarendon English Series. Each volume contains a representative selection from the works of one author, prefaced by the best critical essays (or extracts) dealing with his writings, and a brief introduction designed to supplement these essays and bring them into focus. The selections are annotated. Crown 8vo. 3s. 6d. each. The series includes the following volumes :—

> *Bacon, Borrow, Burke, Cobbett, Coleridge, Cowper, De Quincey, Dryden, Fielding, Goldsmith, Gray, Johnson, Keats, Charles Lamb, Milton, More, Spenser, Wordsworth.* Volumes on *Chaucer, Fuller,* and *Burns* are in the press.

Shakespeare's Plays, edited with introduction and notes, by G. S. Gordon. Crown 8vo. Cloth. 2s. each.

> *As You Like It, Coriolanus, Hamlet, Julius Caesar, Macbeth, A Midsummer Night's Dream, Richard II, The Tempest, Twelfth-Night.*

Shakespeare's Plays, edited with introduction and notes by W. G. Clark and W. Aldis Wright. Fcap 8vo. Stiff paper covers, 2s. 6d. each, except *The Merchant of Venice*, 2s.

> *As You Like It, Coriolanus, Hamlet, Henry IV Part I, Henry V, Henry VIII, Julius Caesar, King John, King Lear, Macbeth, The Merchant of Venice, A Midsummer Night's Dream, Much Ado About Nothing, Richard II, Richard III, The Tempest, Twelfth-Night.*

Lists of the above Series may be had on application to the

OXFORD UNIVERSITY PRESS

Amen House, London, E.C. 4